2004

ONCE UPON A RHYME

IMAGINATION FOR A NEW GENERATION

Worcestershire

Edited by Claire Tupholme

 Young**Writers**

First published in Great Britain in 2004 by:
Young Writers
Remus House
Coltsfoot Drive
Peterborough
PE2 9JX
Telephone: 01733 890066
Website: www.youngwriters.co.uk

SB ISBN 1 84460 464 0

Foreword

Young Writers was established in 1991 and has been passionately devoted to the promotion of reading and writing in children and young adults ever since. The quest continues today. Young Writers remains as committed to engendering the fostering of burgeoning poetic and literary talent as ever.

This year's Young Writers competition has proven as vibrant and dynamic as ever and we are delighted to present a showcase of the best poetry from across the UK. Each poem has been carefully selected from a wealth of *Once Upon A Rhyme* entries before ultimately being published in this, our twelfth primary school poetry series.

Once again, we have been supremely impressed by the overall high quality of the entries we have received. The imagination, energy and creativity which has gone into each young writer's entry made choosing the best poems a challenging and often difficult but ultimately hugely rewarding task - the general high standard of the work submitted amply vindicating this opportunity to bring their poetry to a larger appreciative audience.

We sincerely hope you are pleased with our final selection and that you will enjoy *Once Upon A Rhyme Worcestershire* for many years to come.

Contents

Tom Dunn (11)	18
Samuel Ransome-Williams (7)	18
Flora Henderson (9)	19
Joe Watts (8)	19
Philippa Jolliffe (9)	20
Lydia Garfield (11)	20
William Dee (10)	21
Tom Green (10)	21
Luke Humphreys (10)	22

Holy Redeemer Primary School

Rebecca Harker (9)	22
Adele Heathcote (9)	23
Jade McKillup (9)	23
Alice Winters (9)	24
Ruth Pollard (8)	24
Isobel Fallon (8)	25
James Mattey (9)	25
Rosie Ludlow (8)	25
Jessica Tarran (8)	26
Patrick Harrison (9)	26
Connie Archer (9)	27
Katherine Danckert (8)	27
Charlie Crawford (8)	28
Emily Taylor (8)	28
Hannah Grubb (8)	29
Hannah Evans (8)	29
Keely Hewlett (8)	30
Stephen Lockie (9)	30
Lucy Ellingworth (8)	31
Sean Kerr (9)	31

Madresfield CE Primary School

Yasmin Jones (8)	31
Jodie Coates (8)	32
Bethany Moore (9)	32
Sophie Bird (8)	33
William Hughes (9)	33
Rebecca Owen (9)	34
Laura Morton (7)	34
Matthew Wall (7)	34

Tegan McBeth (8)	35
Ellen De Santis (8)	35
Anna Mullins (8)	35
James Rance (8)	36
Beth Smith (8)	36
Charlotte Pinkney (8)	37
Luke Smith (8)	37
Rachel Price (8)	38
Jack Mackintosh (8)	38
Emilie Stephens (8)	39
Owen Hodges (7)	39

Northleigh CE Primary School

Erin Cunningham (10)	40
Emma Knowles (9)	40
Helena Dixon (10)	41
Hayley Roberts (11)	41
James Morrison (11)	42
Tom MacKenzie (11)	42
Sophie Dawson (10)	43
Amy Plumstead (10)	43
Rebecca Lockton (8)	44
William Baker (8)	44
Amelia Arnold (10)	44
Rhian Alford (11)	45
Isobel Mathias (9)	45
Jai Flanagan (10)	46
Sam March (9)	46
Ben Hodgkiss (11)	47
Jodie Bannister (10)	47
Georgia Visser (10)	48
Ben Davenport (11)	48
Charlotte Jakeman (9)	49
Bradley Morton (10)	49
Declan Amphlett (7)	50
Stuart Puffett (10)	50
Joe Brooker (9)	51
Frances Purnell (10)	51
Myles Cunningham (9)	52
Tom Milner (9)	52
Josh Williams (10)	53

Fern Dawson (7)	54
Matthew Green (9)	54
Rowan Whitehouse (8)	55
Jamie MacKenzie (8)	55
Victoria Dexter (8)	56
Philip Weatherill (9)	56
Jack Richards (10)	57
Rachel Martin (9)	57
Alexandra Smith (9)	58
Jake Stromqvist (8)	58
Matthew Wren (9)	59
Hannah Kenyon (9)	60
Jessica Smith (9)	60
Megan Hickling (9)	61
Amy Straughan (9)	61
Nicholas Wilson (11)	61
Frankie Shackleton (9)	62
Robert Derrington (10)	62
Vanessa Macdonald (9)	62
Caryn Bristow (10)	63
Cameron Heaton (8)	63
Isabel Massey (9)	64
Pippa Lewis (9)	64
Abigail Smith (11)	64
Charlie Bytheway (9)	65
Lucy Cooper (8)	65
Bethaney Allbright (11)	65

St Nicholas CE Middle School, Pinvin

Grace Harker (11)	66
Joanna Train (10)	66
Alec Smith (10)	67
Alice Nicklin (10)	67
Sebastian Shaw (11)	68
Sophie Edwards (10)	68
Ryan Perks (10)	69
Charlotte Ruff (10)	69
Josh Sutterby (11)	70
Francesca Gordon (10)	70
Fred Simmons (10)	71
Jessica Morris (11)	71

Rebecca Lear (10)	72
Hannah Downs (11)	72
Thomas Neal (10)	73
Rebecca East (10)	73
Lily Barrett (10)	74
Lara Smith (9)	74
Victoria Woolley (11)	75
Sam Evan White-Edwards (10)	75
Jessica Smith (10)	76
Millie Boddy (10)	76
Lucy Hanson (10)	77
Lucy Taylor (9)	77
Rachel Corbett (10)	78
Katie Hickinbotham (10)	78
Jessica Hawthorn (9)	79
Diane Barker (9)	79
Hector Davies (10)	80
Eleanor Britton (10)	80
Alasdair McGillivray (10)	81
Olivia A Wiles (9)	81
Jaeren Coathup (9)	82
Myles Weaver (9)	82
Felicity Parkinson-Allsopp (9)	83
Olivia Hartley (9)	83
Joshua Lawton (9)	84
Luke Sephton (10)	84
Jessica Sykes (10)	85
Steph McStay (10)	85
Jo Gaze (10)	86
Abigail Pallett (9)	86
Daniel Spencer (9)	87
Abigail Jones (10)	87
Kelly Ryder (10)	88
Josh Critchley (10)	88
Harry Mallinson (10)	89
Ellie Morris (9)	89
Megan Heeks (11)	90
Georgie Bailey (10)	91
Chris Billingham (10)	91

Stanley Road Primary School

Christopher Butcher-Calderón & James Michael Smith (10)	92
Lucy Hencher	92
Aumair Qayum (10)	93
Amy Bull (11)	93

The Mount School

Ryan Sanders-Fox (11)	94
Hannah Duffey (10)	95
Jack Newman (10)	95
James Higginbottom (10)	96
Jack Sims (11)	96
Ryan Hughes (10)	97
Kyle Ashworth (9)	97
Dominic Denton (10)	98
Stephanie Hosking (10)	98
Oliver Hughes-Clarke (9)	99
Ashley Downes (9)	99
Charlotte Roden (9)	99
Bethan Winter (9)	100
Robert Lee (10)	101
William Tresidder (8)	102
Jack Pendlebury (9)	102
Ga Kei Sin (9)	102
Alhasan Alhabib (9)	103
Lloyd Raybone (10)	103
Lauren Bhaduri (9)	104
Laurence Denton (10)	104
Fern Share (9)	105

Upton Upon Severn CE Primary School

Chloe Sharpe (8)	105
Elena Ioannou (9)	106
Emily Gregory (8)	106
Daniel Hopkins (9)	107
Cody Stokes (9)	107
Sarah Hopkins (9)	108
Billy Taylor (8)	108
Jack Marklew (10)	109
Laura Morgan (8)	109

Nathan Parsons (10)	110
Jim Owen (9)	110
Emily Jade Gould (10)	111
Elliott Dawe (9)	112
Ryan Westbrook (10)	112
Michelle Lockyear (10)	113
Jessica Short (10)	113
Jessica Hewlett (10)	114
Josh Barnett (9)	115
Annabelle Dodd (8)	116
James Breeze-Stringfellow (8)	116
James Treacy (8)	117
George Chapman (8)	117
Korinna Barnard (8)	118
Matthew Burt (8)	118
Tom Bottomley (9)	119
Hannah Barney (7)	119
Kayleigh Dodd (10)	120
Sophie Swann (8)	120
Sophie-Marie Price (8)	121
Rebecca Chamberlain (8)	121
Kelsey Bannister (8)	122
Carianne Martin (10)	122
Chantelle Parsons (8)	123
Ryan Hill (7)	123
Laurence James Astill (8)	124
Bryn Jarvis (8)	124
Martha Owen (8)	125
Hannah Broadbent (7)	125
Dale Willis (10)	125
Kara Beth Thomas (9)	126
Jessica Williams (8)	126
Georgie McMullen (8)	127
Jacob Jones (8)	127
William St Leger-Chambers (8)	128
Hannah Simmons (7)	128
William Cullwick (9)	129
Samantha Dewick (8)	129
Rhiannon Turner (9)	130
Yoseph Taha (8)	130
Bethany Cooper (8)	131
Amy Miles (7)	131

Matthew Bromwich (10)	132
George Dawe (7)	132
Oliver Storr (8)	133
Alfie Owen (7)	133
Alister Stevens (9)	134
Tim Lewis (7)	134
Bethan Howells (8)	135
Anthony Miles (7)	135

Winterfold House School

Harry Maher (9)	136
Jo Dearden (10)	136
Annie Jenkinson (9)	137
Charlie Muir (9)	137
Charlie Green (10)	138
Harry Nuttall (10)	138
Ginny Brewer (9)	139
Tim Atkinson (10)	139
Julien Petitjean (10)	140
Kate Robbins (9)	140
Alex Willson (10)	141
Nicholas Radcliffe (10)	141
Belle Watson (10)	142
Alex Attwood (10)	142
Duncan Keir (10)	143
Olivia Foulds (9)	143
Max Hunter (10)	144
Jonathan Newbould (7)	144
Daniel El-Dalil (11)	145
Georgia Warner Tomlinson (8)	145
Rupert Buchanan (10)	146
Grace Stringer (8)	146
Harriet Alford (10)	147
Joshua Passmore (9)	147
Fiona McHugh (11)	148
Danny Kalloghlian (8)	148
Tom Westley (10)	149
James Thornton (11)	149
Jessica Dunn (8)	150
Elizabeth Hawkley (11)	151
Abbie-May Griffiths (8)	152

Witton Middle School

The Poems

Miss Butler And Her Chapatti Machine

Once upon a time I had a dream
About Miss Butler and her chapatti machine
Miss Butler wore the hat of a baker
And wished she was an expert chapatti maker
But Miss Butler's chapatti making was bad
So she made a machine out of things that she had.

When it was made she pressed the green button
It started off slowly, then all of a sudden
Got faster and louder and started to roar
And then it sped up just a little bit more
The sound was as if the kitchen would break
And just then, the machine, it started to shake.

While Miss Butler watched in pure amazement
People gathered on the pavement
And stared in through the open window
People watched there below
The machine had started throwing out
Chapattis everywhere about.

The best chapattis ever tasted
So they would never ever be wasted
It even put them onto plates
So Miss Butler showed it to all of her mates
Miss Butler took off her baker's hat
Now the machine makes chapattis for aristocrats.

Farrah Nawaz (10)

A Boy Called Fred

There once was a redhead called Fred,
He had an extremely large head,
He fell out of a tree,
His sister jumped with glee,
Until she was sent up to bed.

Frederick Williams (11)
Abberley Hall School

My Form Room

In my form room
There is an alien in the cupboard
A snake under the chairs
The pens and rulers have battles
But really no one cares.

The TV has sprouted legs
And the board pen is being rude
The rubbers are dancing
The mice are eating pencils as food.

The felt tips are doing drawings
The crayons colouring it in
The lockers have started talking
And the glue stick kicked my shin.

The stapler is being a bully
The books are flying away
The windows are crushing the paint box
The teacher walking in, nothing to say.

Serena North (11)
Abberley Hall School

Senses Of Snow

Glistening is the beautiful snow floating to the ground,
All you hear is your heart beating, pound, pound, pound,
All you see is children running round, round, round,
Lots of little snowmen are now little mounds.

Frosty is the gleaming snow freezing in the sky,
Mum is cooking hot food, pie, pie, pie,
Everyone's stopped throwing snowballs, why? Why? Why?
Snow is melting fast now, bye, bye, bye.

Amy Hiles (10)
Abberley Hall School

Kennings About A Dog

House racer
Rabbit chaser

Tail shaker
Cat food taker

Shoe biter
Toy fighter

Sofa snoozer
Hair loser

Car rider
Ball hider

Meat cruncher
Biscuit muncher

Bed sleeper
Trouble getting deeper

Zip breaker
Hair flaker.

George Shirlaw (11)
Abberley Hall School

A Box Of Senses

A box of senses was delivered through my door
I went over and started to lift up the lid.
There was Cowardice shying away in the corner.
Happiness flew away down the road.
Beauty skipped round my head as Sadness slinked away.
Hatred rose up and hit me on the nose then ran quickly out the door.
Bravery jumped out the box and he ran after Hatred
And Gentleness plaited my hair.
Joy laughed loudly then sat by the fire
And Laziness slept on the sofa.

Lauren Craigen (11)
Abberley Hall School

An Unhealthy Diet

Fridge tracker
Chocolate snacker

Biscuit taker
Tummy acher

Sweet tooth
Honey booth

Ice cream muncher
Malteaser cruncher

Coke drinker
Cake thinker

Fat food desire
Burger buyer

Fruit and veg hater
Big tummy maker

One fat slob.

Toby Free (10)
Abberley Hall School

A Weird Woman Limerick

There once was a girl with a beard,
Her face was ever so weird,
She then had a child,
It was extremely wild
And now it is always feared.

Bertie Wilson (11)
Abberley Hall School

Seasons Poem

In the summer flowers grow
And a little breeze will blow,
Animals bringing up their young,
They play around and bathe in sun.

In the autumn full of rain,
Squirrels like to play a game,
Scurry around and fetch some nuts,
So they will enjoy winter much.

In the winter snow will come,
Children playing and have much fun,
Making snowmen all day long,
With birds singing their winter song.

In the spring buds will come,
Bringing showers and a little sun,
Blossom growing, daffodils flowing,
Bringing fun for everyone.

Sarah Weaving (10)
Abberley Hall School

There Was An Old Man Called Bob

There was an old called Bob
He once sat on the hob
He yelped in pain
And ran down the lane
What a silly old man called Bob.

Sam Pinson (11)
Abberley Hall School

The Giant Woodlouse

There once was a giant woodlouse,
Who lived in a very small house,
He tried to get in
And fell into the bin,
The silly, old, giant woodlouse.

The woodlouse crawled out of the bin
And he kicked up a terrible din,
The neighbours attacked
And he drove them all back,
The powerful, old, giant woodlouse.

The woodlouse found some elastic
And made something 'quite fantastic',
He pulled on a strand,
The house was going to expand,
The clever, old, giant woodlouse.

James Spicer (10)
Abberley Hall School

Hunting

The old fox lying in the grass,
he hears the horses galloping, pass.

The clattering hooves whooshing past,
tails flapping like an old ship's mast.

The hounds pick up his scent,
on his feet the fox went.

They have a plot,
the gun shot.

Bang . . . silence.

Amelia Flower (10)
Abberley Hall School

My Family Is Mad

My brother is mad
He sat on my dad
He's been cheeky since he was born,
Then one night
He suffered a fright
He was rolling around on the floor.

My sister is mad
This makes me glad
She always takes the blame,
She smirks with glee
At my brother and me
She always takes the blame, what a shame.

My dad is mad
This is bad
He drives me crazy
He smells like a daisy,
We call him Slow Norris
Or sometimes Big Borris
He is seriously mad.

My mum is mad
But she loves my dad
I think she's great
She likes chilli and rice
And all things nice
And is never ever late.

But . . . as for me
I'm perfect!

Jack Prevett (11)
Abberley Hall School

Owl Kennings

Night waker
Rodent taker

Eyes wider
Worm hider

Mice snatcher
Rat catcher

Head spinner
Shrew dinner

Wise thinker
Eye winker

Day snoozer
Bad loser

Loud tweeter
Frog eater

Air soarer
Food lurer.

Alastair Higgins (11)
Abberley Hall School

Creature Comforts

F rogs are slimy and very small,
R ipply skin and squidgy toes.
O n twelve toes they crawl,
G eckos think they're crazy,
S nakes are jealous because they're cool.

L izards are long and look like iguanas,
I t swims around like some piranhas,
Z e French think they're mad
A nd the Swiss think they're bad,
R eally they're mean
D o they ever clean?
S o that's that.

William Barnes (9)
Cradley Primary School

Over Hell

Over there, the chalk
explodes like
entire dynamite.
Over here, the bats
bomb like a
Spitfire swooping
at midnight.
Over hell, the
blood drips from
a gold and silver
sword charging
into battle.
Inside Heaven, the
bunnies jump like a
person on a space hopper
on top of a trampoline.
Heading for death, a
person on a sledge
heading straight for
a tree.

Richard Smith (9)
Cradley Primary School

Hamster

A hamster is a cuddly creature
You can cuddle them
But sometimes they scratch
They nibble your fingers
They fill their pouches with food
They wake up at night.

George Banner (10)
Cradley Primary School

My Basset Hound

I had a basset hound,
He cost me a whole one hundred pound.
But one day he broke his back,
He got stuck in a sack.

My basset had long ears,
He always had tears.
He always drank beers,
He always ran along piers.

But I got a new basset hound,
That cost me three hundred pound.
He always licks you
And one day I took him to the zoo.

Matthew Walford (10)
Cradley Primary School

Tiger Trouble And Bunny Bouncing

T igers need food and prey,
 I gnoring tigers upsets them,
G ood tigers wouldn't attack humans,
E very tiger has stripes,
R oaring tigers are mad at that moment,
S outhern India has hardly any tigers.

R abbits bounce in a funny way,
A rabbit can nibble a jumper a lot,
B aby rabbits are all fluffy and cute,
B unny rabbits are very fierce,
 I t purrs at me,
T alking to my rabbit is hard,
S eeing my rabbit hop is sweet.

Chloe Hardwick (9)
Cradley Primary School

Hamsters

Little hamster
Scurries around,
Jumps off platforms,
Climbing up bars,
One by one.
Little zoomer
Slidding around
Sniffing around,
Jumping about
Nibbling food.
When he's tired he's weak
He does one more jump
And falls.
Falls lower and lower
Until a little tiny thump,
Before going to bed
In the morning.

William Cooper (8)
Cradley Primary School

Cats

Cats are big, cats are small,
Some clever and some are not,
Some are black and some are white,
Some don't like playing at night,
Some are fat and some are thin,
But my cat's called Brin,
He's not a fat cat,
He's thin!

Harry Hathaway (9)
Cradley Primary School

I Am A Guinea Pig

If you saw a guinea pig and you thought
It was mean, you have not seen me!

I nibble like a lightning bolt!
I drink like a vacuum!
I sniff like a piggy pig, pigging in his home!
I sleep like a mouse!
And if that is not enough
I will tell you more!

My eyes are like hearts frightfully glowing!
My toes are like cushions!
My nose is big and plump!
My ears are like snowflakes!
My tail (if it existed) would be
As if it was a piece of rice!

But enough of me, what about you?
Are you fiercer or hairier than me,
Sugar Plum the guinea pig?

Victoria Collins (10)
Cradley Primary School

Dolphins

D ipping in water
O ver the surface
L eaping over me
P lopping into the surface
H opping out from the water
 I solated in Antarctica
N ipping my hand
S oaked in water.

Louis Powell (9)
Cradley Primary School

Death

Rumbling, rumbling, rumbling in the distance,
Crumbling, crumbling, crumbling from the ground.
Graves explode in a Fulham graveyard.
Rotting zombies rise from the ground.

Rumbling, rumbling, rumbling in the distance,
Crumbling, crumbling, crumbling from the ground.
Hideous faces with eyeless sockets,
Deformed bodies with gruesome legs.

Rumbling, rumbling, rumbling in the distance,
Crumbling, crumbling, crumbling from the ground.
Dead men bring death to anyone in their way,
They kill, they hack, they chop off heads.
Beware . . . death is coming!

Max Waters (10)
Cradley Primary School

Dolphins

Dolphins! Dolphins! Lovely things
They're always on the go!
They have silver fins
They jump high and low.

Oh dolphins! Dolphins! Lovely things
They're always on the go!
It looks like they have wings
I call him Flo!

Dolphins! Dolphins! Lovely things
They're always on the go!
Pretending to be king,
His best friend is Jo!

Lauren Munrowd (8)
Cradley Primary School

The Shark Song

Neither guns nor radars have I
But I have razor-sharp fins, a big wide mouth
And I have . . .
Teeth, teeth, teeth!

Neither venom nor stings have I
But I have a ferocious stare
And I have . . .
Teeth, teeth, teeth!

Freddy van Vuren (7)
Cradley Primary School

For Naomi

My dad is the kind of dad who . . .
Washes in the shower all day
Wiggles the car on the way to Spain
Sings in the shower
He's always late from work
Hopeless at diving in the swimming pool
And he always says, 'no'.

Peter Bennett (7)
Cradley Primary School

Urban Storm

The wind batters the buildings like a battering ram
And the waves crash up the streets, someone screams.
Hunting the people as if they are prey, small and weak.
Families struggle alone, fearing the cold and the dark.
Suddenly through the roaring of the storm
There's the sound of cracking steel
Then a shattering of glass as a skyscraper falls; then another.
They cannot bear the strain of the storm's beating.

Mark Adair (10)
Cradley Primary School

Plants And Trees

The trees rustle as gentle winds blow,
Back and forth.
Trees and plants whisper to each other
In a calm way.

While peacefully in a quiet wood
Lavender sprinkles its pollen
Over damp, mossy ground.

In the Queen's garden
Gardeners weed and work,
Day and night,
To let beautiful flowers bloom,
To make it lovely.

Everywhere plants are growing,
Dying,
Reproducing,
That's life!

Lizzie Barnes (11)
Cradley Primary School

Cheetah

Cheetah, cheetah
Ever so fast
And really slick
As he moves scattering the dust.
He runs through the jungle like a bullet
When he lies
He stretches his legs out and his body.
You think that he is asleep
But he is actually awake
His eyes are actually open
A teeny-weeny bit.

Joshua Banner (7)
Cradley Primary School

Not Quite My Favourite Teddy

In the peace and quiet and safety of bed,
There lyeth a sleeping ted,
One ear is torn, one leg is bent,
(That is, until to bed you are sent).

And then he awakes, to haunt your dreams,
To shatter your sleep,
Make useless trash
Of counting sheep.

A vengeful nightmare dear teddy becomes,
But a light seeps through; the dawn incomes.
And this may happen, (just you wait),
If, just once, you stay up . . .
Too late!

Abigail Downie (11)
Cradley Primary School

Horses

Horses gallop
round and round
like a never-ending circle,
they gallop in the street
she gallops through the wild wind
with her mane blowing
behind her.
She glides through the wind
like a sail boat.
She's 5 foot tall
and 3 foot l-o-n-g!

Emily Francis (7)
Cradley Primary School

For Naomi

My dad is the kind of dad who . . .
Wants to quit work
Wastes time
Hates driving
Tries handbrake turns around corners
Bites his nails until they go blank
Sings like mad in the car
Puts hair gel on and always makes us late for school
And he always burns sausages so they taste horrible
Tries to check the time when he's starving
Tries to build an extension
And does horrible writing
And sounds like Scooby-Doo!

Alexi Gregory (8)
Cradley Primary School

For Naomi

My dad is the kind of dad who . . .

Sings in the street
Cuts himself shaving
Has music too loud
Eats all our chocolate
Has his hair cut at the last minute
Is lazy
Always late
Cuts his nails too short
Sings in the car
Adds words to stories

Oh no! But I love him so.

Lydia Parkhill (8)
Cradley Primary School

Man's Destruction Of Nature

Trees rustle contentedly,
As gentle breezes whisper to its leaves,
So peaceful.

Monkeys natter sociably,
Contemplating yesterday's fight,
So peaceful.

Squirrels scuttle busily,
Preparing seasoned acorns,
So peaceful.

Humans chainsaw down the trees,
While a tiny rabbit whimpers at his dead mother's side,
So evil.

Factories start their murderous life,
While the last fox cub keels over dead,
So tragic.

Tom Dunn (11)
Cradley Primary School

Predators

Leopards and tigers, lions too,
Hunting the wildlife that they like to chew,
Peregrine falcons in the air
Catching mice as a dare.
Snakes and lizards in the trees
Slithering and scampering in the breeze,
Grey wolf, sparrow hawk too
Running and gliding for food,
Praying mantis, tiger shark too
Swimming and crawling for food.

Samuel Ransome-Williams (7)
Cradley Primary School

The Jet-Black Horse

In a sunny meadow,
Stands a jet-black horse.
Grazing under the cool shade
Of a large chestnut tree.
As the gentle wind blows,
The tree whistles and shakes
Its branches.
In the sudden coldness
The horse shivers
Like a freezer.
A girl comes to the gate
With a bucket of feed -
Let it eat!
Let it eat!
Let it eat!

Flora Henderson (9)
Cradley Primary School

For Naomi

My dad is the kind of dad who . . .

Hoofs the ball into the field.
Jacuzzi's in the bath.
Sings with the radio.
Pulls my leg to wake me up.
Is mad about West Bromwich Albion FC.
Argues with Mum.
And . . .
Shouts really loud!
But I love my dad!

Joe Watts (8)
Cradley Primary School

Guardian Angel

On a sandy bay at the dead of night
A horse gracefully rears as if it wants to fly away
He runs to the sea and lays down wishing to be home in Canada
He wants to be in a dream far far away
He's so confused he sees a guardian angel
Coming to whisk him away for evermore
His dream is coming true . . .

He leaps over the moon, rears with the stars,
And then he closes his eyes and sleeps on a cloud
He's so happy he can't be hurt, he can't be worked.
Then he drifts away back to the world then he awakens,
He feels bubbly and happy like air
Then he gets up and rears always to feel and know
He has a guardian angel watching him always.

Philippa Jolliffe (9)
Cradley Primary School

Food Fight

And they're off, piling onto tables, food flying everywhere!
Alice's yoghurt's spilt again,
Philippa jumps into a spare space before James,
Vicky halfway through her lunch, with Naomi still on her sandwich.

Oh no! Dominic's ice-skating on Tom's banana skin,
Harry spilt his drink over Oliver!
Lizzie catapults her cake at the teacher, splat!
The dinner ladies can't bear to watch anymore. They quit,
The headmistress flies through the door trying to stop it all,
It doesn't work. What a disappointment! There's a food fight.

Lydia Garfield (11)
Cradley Primary School

The Dragon

When the dragon comes to your home
Run! Run! Run!
If he returns to his dingy den,
Phew! Phew! Phew!
The dragon soars over the treetops,
Eating all to see.
Dare you go to the dragon's den?
Rather you than me!
The dragon soars over fresh water seas,
Fishing under the blue.
Will you return from the dragon's den?
Rather me than you!

William Dee (10)
Cradley Primary School

All The Day

Keep your pants on,
All the day,
So you can play
And keep the bath away.

Keep your pants on,
All the day,
So you can play
To keep the chill away.

Keep your pants on,
All the day,
So you run away
And keep the girls away.

Tom Green (10)
Cradley Primary School

Ice Cream

When I went to the ice cream shop
They had lots of different flavours
Like marvellous mint,
Super, succulent strawberry,
Raving, raspberry ripple,
Choking chocolate chip
And Chinese chilli,
I love ice cream,
It makes me scream,
Strawberry my favourite flavour
And I tease my next-door neighbour.

Luke Humphreys (10)
Cradley Primary School

Best Friends

Funny
Cool
Kind
Pretty
Josie is my best friend
Cute
Clever
Wears a dress
Smart
Josie is my best friend
Listens
Talks a lot
Good
Kind
Josie is my best friend.

Rebecca Harker (9)
Holy Redeemer Primary School

Jade

Generous
friendly
sincere
clever
funny
Jade's special to me!
Listens
laughs
kind
pretty
sparkles
Jade's special to me!
Cute
smart
best pal
Jade's special to me!

Adele Heathcote (9)
Holy Redeemer Primary School

My Best Friend

Her hair is as clean as the sea
Her eyes sparkle like a star
And when she smiles
Her lips gleam like a shadow
She makes me laugh with surprise
Her hair waves around
Like the world is coming to her
She giggles to the moon
She laughs and laughs
And makes my heart go apart.

Jade McKillup (9)
Holy Redeemer Primary School

100% Naughty

Naughty, naughtier, naughtiest
Naughtiest girl in town
I really should wear a crown
For being the best of the naughties
Even if I am in my forties.

Naughty, naughtier, naughtiest
Naughtiest girl in class
I smashed the glass
Messed about in maths
And overflowed the baths.

Naughty, naughtier, naughtiest
Naughtiest girl around
I make an awful sound
Get the little kids drowned
And give teachers an awful pound.

Naughty, naughtier, naughtiest
Naughtiest girl in school
Of course I'm a fool
You must have guessed I am a teacher
A wonderful feature
But also 100% naughty.

Alice Winters (9)
Holy Redeemer Primary School

Penguins

We waddle about on our icebergs
Which make our feet slither and slide,
And when we get close to the water
We leap with a splash off the side!

Ruth Pollard (8)
Holy Redeemer Primary School

My Best Friend

Emily has . . .
Hair as blonde as the sun.
Her eyes are as blue as the sea.
Her smile is as big as the world.
I know she's a friend to me.

Isobel Fallon (8)
Holy Redeemer Primary School

My Best Friend

He always makes me laugh
He has lots of voices
He's a true friend to me

He always helps when I'm sad
He's never in a mood
He asks me if I want to play a game with him
He's a true friend to me.

James Mattey (9)
Holy Redeemer Primary School

My Best Mate

I have a lot of good friends at Holy Redeemer School
but my very best mate is Jessie of course
she is kind and so small
her eyes are bright blue.

It's easy to spot when she's out in the cold
it's true she's hard working most of the time
that's my best friend, now off we go.

Rosie Ludlow (8)
Holy Redeemer Primary School

I Love Jelly

I love jelly
Jelly is fantastic
Jelly is wobbly
Jelly is sometimes cold
Jelly comes in strawberry
Orange and blackcurrant flavour.
Lovely.
Jelly is red, orange
And black colour.
That's nice.
I love jelly in my belly.
Jelly makes me feel like jelly.
Jelly makes my tummy
Feel very cold
Even my head.
I love jelly!

Jessica Tarran (8)
Holy Redeemer Primary School

Loose Windows

I will take, I the wind,
I will roar, I will whistle.

Tiles rattling,
I will smash, I the wind,
I will roar, I will whistle.

Leaves wandering,
I will scatter, I the wind,
I will roar, I will whistle.

Hay blowing,
I will suck, I the wind,
I will roar, I will whistle.

Patrick Harrison (9)
Holy Redeemer Primary School

Meg

Joyful
Fun
Clever
Mad
Meg is a true friend to me.
Funny
Loopy
Busted fan
Loud
Meg is the best friend there can be.
Messy
Loving
Kind
Friendly
I miss Meg as can be.

Connie Archer (9)
Holy Redeemer Primary School

Emily

Generous
laughing
she's my best friend
funny
kind
she's my best friend
sincere
talks
she's my best friend
cries
listens
she's my bestest ever friend.

Katherine Danckert (8)
Holy Redeemer Primary School

Best Friends

Kind,
Funny,
Generous,
Sweet,
Laughs.
My best friend is a true friend to me.
Chases,
Makes up games,
Bright,
Shining,
Like a star,
Like the sun.
My best friend is a true friend to me.
Sparkles,
Glistens,
Never lies,
Never fights,
Always wants to play,
Always comes round to my house,
My best friend is a true friend to me.

Charlie Crawford (8)
Holy Redeemer Primary School

My Best Friend

I have lots of friends but here's one for you
her name is Molly though she has left school too.
I see her quite a lot on Saturdays and Sundays.
I go for sleepovers there, and have laughs too.
I like her very much because she has a nice smile.
She laughs with me and we have great times together.
My best friend Molly, she has blonde hair
and fair hair just like me.
She comes to my parties too.
She is my best friend of all.

Emily Taylor (8)
Holy Redeemer Primary School

Emily

Nice
Generous
Gives
Talks
She's my best friend and always.

Kind-hearted
Cares
Laughs
Funny
She's my best friend and always.

Listens
Sincere
We agree
Chasing each other
She's my best friend and always.

Bratz
Sleepover Club
My scene.
She's my friend.
She's my best friend and always.

Hannah Grubb (8)
Holy Redeemer Primary School

I've Got Pets

I've got dogs
I've got a cat
I've got a mouse under the mat
I've got a Shetland
I've got a chick
I've got a snake that makes me sick
And I've got a spider that drinks cider
I've got an insect
All of them live with me!

Hannah Evans (8)
Holy Redeemer Primary School

Best Friends

B est friends are true friends
E very morning we meet up in the playground.
S tay at each other's house at night.
T reat each other with presents.

F riends together all the time.
R est of our lives
I will be there for the rest of our lives.
E very day we play together
N ight and day we are together
D ay spent just playing together
S ee you tomorrow.

Keely Hewlett (8)
Holy Redeemer Primary School

Animal Poem

Ever seen
a goat
on a boat?

Ever seen
a baboon
in a spoon?

Ever seen
a cat
being fat?

Ever seen
a dog
snog?

Stephen Lockie (9)
Holy Redeemer Primary School

Ruth

Ruth is kind and loving
also funny and playful.
Ruth is generous and helpful
she's a lovely friend to have.
Ruth is joyful and sincere
also listens and is always here.
Ruth is chatty and pretty
she's a lovely friend to have.

Lucy Ellingworth (8)
Holy Redeemer Primary School

Chocolate

I wake up in the middle of the night
I hear a rumble and it's quite a fright
I jump out of bed, I creep down the stairs,
The fridge, I can't stop now,
I open the door, the lights come on,
It's Mum. 'You're grounded!' she shouted.

Sean Kerr (9)
Holy Redeemer Primary School

My View

The moon's a huge white netball,
The sun's a golden penny.
The stars are shimmering bottle tops,
The planets are a box of Smarties, spilt across the sky.
The world is whizzing round and round
And I'm a little devil.

Yasmin Jones (8)
Madresfield CE Primary School

Daphne, Little Dancer

Daphne, little dancer is going out to dance.
She is so good at ballet, she is starting to twirl and prance.
Her friend sees her whirling and starts to do it too.
Then along comes her teacher. Her name is Miss Lu-Lu.
Miss Lu-Lu says, 'Stop now girls, one of you may fall.'
Daphne, little dancer sees more friends over the wall.

Daphne, little dancer shouts, 'Come and dance with me.'
'Sorry!' say her friends, 'we need to have our tea.'
Daphne, little dancer, walks sadly to her house,
There aren't any noises, not even the quiet of a mouse.
Then Daphne, little dancer, has a super idea,
This will make all of her friends cheer!
She is going to try a new dance, this one called 'tap'.
But Daphne, little dancer, needs first to take a nap!

Daphne, little dancer, sets off to her new class,
But, down by the river, her ankle went crash!
Her friends, realised, she needed some fun.
They all cried together, 'Daphne needs a chum!'
They thought very carefully and then wrote her a note,
They put it in the river, in a bottle which did float.
Daphne, little dancer, was surprised to find the letter,
But exclaimed, 'They are my friends!' and now I feel much better!

Jodie Coates (8)
Madresfield CE Primary School

It Wasn't Me

It wasn't me who made my dog fat
It wasn't me who made my cat thin
It wasn't me who put the fluff on the floor
It wasn't me who put glue on the door
It wasn't me who made my sisters brats
It wasn't me who bought the rats
It wasn't me who killed the fly . . . but . . .
It was me who said goodbye.

Bethany Moore (9)
Madresfield CE Primary School

Silly Little Jane Lay

Silly little Jane Lay
was born on the ninth of May.
She went out playing one day
with a friend Indigo.
But with her ball she smashed a window
the owner came tramping out.
She rang her mum on the phone,
and all you could hear was a grumbling moan,
so silly Jane Lay did not go there again.
Jane and her friend found another lane,
with all her money she had got
it really was quite a lot
so out she went again
to buy another windowpane.

Sophie Bird (8)
Madresfield CE Primary School

The Little Old Knight

The little knight with a sword of steel,
wanted to eat a takeaway meal.
So he fought two dragons and rode on a camel,
then he washed with a soapy flannel.
He built a tower out of cream,
and broke the world record for dreaming a dream.
He hit the Prime Minister and swallowed a hammer,
then he went off to live in a manor.
He drove a car through the Indian Ocean,
and gave his horse a sleeping potion.
He caught the famous chickenpox,
and got arrested for not ironing socks.
Then that silly old man said, 'Silly old me,
I have to go to a shop to get a nice cup of tea!'

William Hughes (9)
Madresfield CE Primary School

What Is My Pa Like?

My pa is a star,
He never goes in water,
Even though he oughta
He's a bit like a waiter,
I'll tell you about that later.
What is my pa like?
He'd teach you to ride a bike
Or take you for a hike.
But worst of all, he likes to smoke,
What is my pa like?

Rebecca Owen (9)
Madresfield CE Primary School

Wintertime

I love wintertime
when icicles glisten and shine.
It is very dark and bold
my hands are very cold!

I like lots of light
because I like things bright.
It's going to snow
but soon it's going to melt.
Oh no! Oh no! Oh no!

Laura Morton (7)
Madresfield CE Primary School

Snow

It's winter!
You throw slushy snow and you freeze.
It's really fun, you go on a fun sledge.
When the whole world is covered with lovely snow
The pond is as hard as a rock!

Matthew Wall (7)
Madresfield CE Primary School

My Monster

My monster wobbles everywhere . . .
He has moving eyes.
His body is like jelly.
He is very, very funny and he makes people laugh.
He has spiky hair and hands like sticks.
He is purple.

Tegan McBeth (8)
Madresfield CE Primary School

Summertime

Summertime has begun,
I can hear it come.
The sun comes up with a bop,
The moon and stars go with a pop.

I can see a beautiful butterfly fluttering by,
With Fiona the fly they can both fly.
They land on a great big barn,
They lived at the largest farm.

Ellen De Santis (8)
Madresfield CE Primary School

Flowers In The Garden

Flowers in the garden are swishing in the wind.
They look like bright yellow stars.
Some of them are dark red blood
But others are fluttering in the breeze.
Flowers in the garden are as bright as sun!

Anna Mullins (8)
Madresfield CE Primary School

The Dragon

I see the dragon in the distance
moving towards the town,
we can see him swooping down,
we can hear the beating of his wings,
as he moves the town.
His scaly skin is so rough,
we can't shoot him down
because he's too tough.
The dragon is vicious
he thinks I'm delicious
so he heads right down,
pointing towards the town
then in one gulp,
he mashes me to a pulp.

James Rance (8)
Madresfield CE Primary School

Cautionary Tale

The tale of Blubber who ate too much rubber.

There once lived a little boy
He had this terrific toy.
One day he got the toy out
And he gave the most almighty shout.
'Mummy, I'm dying please help!'
Then he gave the biggest blood-curdling yelp!
His parents came indoors, skiing right in,
He put the rubber in his mouth just like a pin.
After his blood turned fiery red,
Then he dropped down on the floor dead!

Moral . . . never give little, dangerous toys
To little silly boys!

Beth Smith (8)
Madresfield CE Primary School

Cheeky Charlie

Cheeky Charlie went out to play
It was a sunny, lovely day
But as soon as she went out
All the kids began to scream and shout
It's cheeky Charlie run away!
I don't want to play with her today
So all the children ran away
So Charlie was left alone in the street
Stamping her own two angry feet.

Then she went home
And sat by her garden gnome
She started to dream
She was in a house made out of cream
Then a wolf made out of bricks
Knocked down a person made out of sticks
She woke up with a start
And found herself in a cart
Well she ran away
For a year and a day
And that's the end of cheeky Charlie
For today!

Charlotte Pinkney (8)
Madresfield CE Primary School

Wishing

There once was a girl called Wishing
That simply loved to go fishing.
She fell into a pond with a shark
Two minutes later it was dark.
Then it was red.
Now she is dead!

Luke Smith (8)
Madresfield CE Primary School

My Friend

My friend is called Jack Sprat,
he's got a very terrible cat.
He comes out at night,
but gives me an awful fright.
He plays tricks on me
you'll see.
He gets me in trouble,
then blows a bubble.
He lies in my bed,
he has an old ted.
His age is nine,
that's just fine.
Jack Sprat lives in my room,
I'm sure you will like to meet him soon.

Rachel Price (8)
Madresfield CE Primary School

Before The Cup Final

Buzzing mind
focus me,
wobbling knees
steady me,
sliding defenders
help us,
scoring strikers
score lots of goals,
diving keeper
save the ball,
applauding subs
cheer us on,
spiky studs
dig into the ground.
Lead me to my goal.

Jack Mackintosh (8)
Madresfield CE Primary School

Wouldn't It Be Funny If You Didn't Have A Nose?

If you didn't have a nose
you couldn't smell a summer rose.
Oh wouldn't it be funny if you didn't have a nose?
When it comes to blow
how would it flow?
If you thought of those who rub their noses
life would be tough for Eskimoses.
Oh wouldn't it be funny if you didn't have a nose?
You couldn't put your glasses on,
they just wouldn't go on.
Oh wouldn't it be funny if you didn't have a nose?
But imagine you fell in muck,
you would still smell yuck
even if you didn't have a nose.

Emilie Stephens (8)
Madresfield CE Primary School

This Morning

I woke up this morning
and heard my dad yawning.
Get dressed
and try to look my best.
Eat breakfast
and my sister is always last.
I am on my way to school,
I am playing with a ball,
now that is all!

Owen Hodges (7)
Madresfield CE Primary School

Midnight

The bats from the belfry wing into the night
Nothing to stop them on their endless flight
The full moon shines down on a chipped Celtic cross
Dusty and musty and covered in moss.
Through the graveyard blows an echoing wind
In and out nooks and crannies it whirls and it spins
Through the whispering willows there blows a cold chill
And suddenly in the graveyard everything is still
My eyes start to shut and as I get weary
My visions get vivid, and weirder and bleary.
A pale-faced vampire draws blood from a tomb
I see a werewolf amidst all the gloom
Seven green monsters all covered in slime
Zombies the colour of an over-ripe lime . . .
I wake up with a jolt, sitting in bed
With a cramp in my foot and a pain in my head
I looked at my clock and gasped at the sight
It was exactly 12 o'clock, midnight!

Erin Cunningham (10)
Northleigh CE Primary School

Murder!

How did you react
When you were attacked?

How did you stagger
When your skin felt the dagger?

How did you cope
Being slung by the rope?

How did you manage
With all that damage?

Why is it always so unfair
That I'm not always ever there?

Emma Knowles (9)
Northleigh CE Primary School

The Titanic

At the bottom of the ocean
There's something you should see,
Mirrors that once reflected the rich,
Now show nothing but seaweed.
Jewels that once sparkled and shined
Now are covered in mud.
Because here is where the greatest ship
Ever built came to a horrible end.

At the bottom of the ocean
There's something you should find,
Dinner suits that were worn for the last time
Now lie tattered and tried.
Chandeliers and candles
That used to light up the ballroom
Sit black and dingy on the rocky sand.
The Titanic on her maiden voyage
Came to a horrible end.
The floating palace sunk here
Never to rise again.

Helena Dixon (10)
Northleigh CE Primary School

Autumn

The air is getting colder
And I am getting older.
The leaves are changing colour
And the sky is getting duller.
The days are getting shorter
And the roads are soaked in water.
Bonfires have started burning
And I am slowly learning.

Hayley Roberts (11)
Northleigh CE Primary School

26 Flippery Fish

A is for American crayfish that don't have a gill
B is for butterfly plax that stay really still
C is for catfish that have a big mouth
D is for dolphin that always swim south
E is for eel that twists like a rubber band
F is for flounder that looks like some sand
G is for gudgeon that swim in a shoal
H is for hatchet fish that are always on patrol
I is for ice cod that swim upside down
J is for jack that wears a frown
K is for killer whale that eats anything
L is for loach that look like rockling
M is for mudskipper that swims in a tank
N is for Nile perch lying under the bank
O is for octopus who never is seen
P is for piranha that is really mean
Q is for quick fry that always gets eaten
R is for ruff that always gets beaten
S is for sun fish that are fat and round
T is for tench that don't make a sound
U is for unusual jellyfish that sting
V is for veilail that has fins like wings
W is for whales that look like sea dinosaurs
X is for extraordinary father lasher that I once saw
Y is for young fish that are Zander's favourite dish
Z is for zebra shark that like eating fish.

James Morrison (11)
Northleigh CE Primary School

There Once Was A Baby From Surrey

There once was a baby from Surrey
Who ate a mountain of curry
He found it too hot
And went back to his cot
And went back to sleep in a hurry.

Tom MacKenzie (11)
Northleigh CE Primary School

Bad Girls

We're rough and we're tough,
And we hate girly stuff,
And the ground we love to scuff.

We rumble and tumble,
Never fall or fumble,
And we scream and we shout and we mumble.

We hate pretty neat frocks,
And black curly locks,
And don't think much of perfumy socks.

We hate diamonds and pearls,
And pretty neat curls,
So as you can see
We're *bad girls!*

Sophie Dawson (10)
Northleigh CE Primary School

Winter's Spell

Leaning trees in the winter breeze,
Death-cold ice and frozen leaves.
Children playing in the snow,
Where does it all come from?
Nobody knows.

Every window sill frosted white,
Whistling winds in the middle of the night.
Lights on the trees and candles in windows,
Snowflakes are falling and telling their story,
Each one has its moment of glory.

Snowball fights in my street,
Lots of turkey for me to eat
And now a fond farewell to everyone
Here under winter's spell.

Amy Plumstead (10)
Northleigh CE Primary School

Animals

I'm a Dalmatian and I run a competition
I'm very spotty and very dotty.

I am a horse, and I use the force
I gallop through the grass and in the daisies
And my friend is called Maizie.

I am a rabbit and I'm bouncy
And I work in the county.

Rebecca Lockton (8)
Northleigh CE Primary School

The Mad Professor And His Hover Car

There, the hover car is coming
They say a mad professor rides it
Every day he passes, we try to say
'Hello,' but instead he gives us sweets
Dogs' bones and cats' milk
Everybody loves the mad professor, I do
So you should too.

William Baker (8)
Northleigh CE Primary School

September!

S ummer's gone, autumn's come,
E veryone is missing the sun,
P iles of leaves on the floor from
T he trees of sycamore.
E veryone is throwing leaves,
M ost people coming for Hallowe'en,
B ut scaring people
E asily.
R emember, remember, the 5th of November.

Amelia Arnold (10)
Northleigh CE Primary School

Peace

No more wars
No more explosions
No more bombing
And cities erosions.

No more crying
Or fighting in the street
No more dying
And seeing armies defeat.

No more, the world
Is rid of fighting
No more do we
Of army sightings.

The people are silent
It's quiet and still
The world is now at peace
But the death toll's past nil.

Rhian Alford (11)
Northleigh CE Primary School

The Dream

Last night in my bed I had a dream,
Of chocolate and crisps and freshly-made ice cream,
I dreamt of a lolly as fat as a house,
I dreamt of a biscuit as small as a mouse,
I dreamt of a gobstopper as big as can be,
I dreamt of a sherbet stick as tall as a tree,
I dreamt of some Smarties which tasted a treat,
I dreamt of some liquorice so juicy and sweet,
But before I could lick it I found that my head,
Had drifted from my dream back into my bed.

Isobel Mathias (9)
Northleigh CE Primary School

Friends All Around

I have a friend called Caryn Bristow,
She likes to eat carrots with Bisto.
My other friend is Georgia Duddy,
She really is my bestest buddy.
The 3rd friend is Natalie Luce,
She's always going on about chocolate mousse.
This is my mad friend, her name is Erin,
She acts like her new pet Herin.
Then next is Katie Harrison,
She doesn't really have much fun.
Then there's Heidi, oh! Heidi, Heidi,
She always ends up breaking her knee.
But last is definitely least, me, Jai, that's my name,
But really that's all I have got to say.
Oh yeah, one more thing, if we go to a different
House or school, we will always be best buddies.

Jai Flanagan (10)
Northleigh CE Primary School

Time Line

Once upon a measly time
When kings and knights drank ale and wine
Stories of murder and betrayal are told
Wars are fought and battles are bold
I look on that and what a bore
Executed if you break the law
Criminals have such a very hard life
Hung, beheaded, your head on a pike
Taste their food and you will bring up
No telling what they drink in a cup
2004 is all good and fine
Now let's look at the medieval time.

Sam March (9)
Northleigh CE Primary School

Tent From Hell

Last night something came into my tent
it was sort of bent
its ears were pricked
and its tail frequently flicked

It climbed on to my bed with a jump
but ended up with a bump
it blew and it hissed
it scratched but it missed

Then I screamed and screamed
it definitely isn't a dream
the very strange creature
was no special feature

Then I reached to turn on the light
it was a sudden delight
it was my wonderful cat
what a relief!

Ben Hodgkiss (11)
Northleigh CE Primary School

Wintertime

W inter flakes all around.
 I n the air and on the ground.
N aughty boys throwing snow.
T hen all the children start to feel low.
E dward's mum making tea.
R ice and chilli for you and me.
T ime for going back out to play.
 I n the snow waiting for Santa's sleigh.
M e and my friend.
E nding the day driving our mums round the bend.

Jodie Bannister (10)
Northleigh CE Primary School

The Class Alphabet

A is for Andrew who punches your arm,
B is for Bertha who lives on a farm,
C is for Clive who picks his nose,
D is for Dot who walks on her toes,
E is for Edward who pushes you over,
F is for Fiona who has a pet cobra,
G is for George who smells like a cow,
H is for Hayley who likes saying 'wow!'
I is for Izaac who eats like a pig,
J is for Joanne who is very big!
K is for Kyle who wants to be a king,
L is for Lucy who destroys everything,
M is for Mike who calls you names,
N is for Norah who likes playing games,
O is for Ollie who loves big cars,
P is for Penelope who has lots of scars,
Q is for Quentin who likes to draw,
R is for Ruby who broke her jaw,
S is for Simon who likes to read books,
T is for Tilly who gets stuck on coat hooks,
U is for Una who gets into trouble,
V is for Vicky who bursts your bubble,
W is for Wellard who kicks you hard,
X is for Xena who would like to get a card,
Y is for Yvonne who is a mess,
Z is for Zoe who always wears a dress.

Georgia Visser (10)
Northleigh CE Primary School

The Rat From Berlin

There was a small rat from Berlin,
Who said, 'I am terribly thin!'
He went to the sales
And bought some scales,
And found he weighed as much as a pin!

Ben Davenport (11)
Northleigh CE Primary School

Rhyme To Rhyme

A is for Arnold who looks like a football.
B is for Bernard who can stop any snowfall.
C is for Clifford who looks like a giant.
D is for Daffy who looks quite a riot.
E is for Elly who is lonely and friendless.
F is for Fred who is not that generous.
G is for Gary who really likes Ron.
H is for Helda who I slammed the door on.
I is for I love cartoons and watch them every day.
J is for Jerry who tries to run away.
K is for Krusty who makes people laugh.
L is for Lisa who once adopted a giraffe.
M is for Mikey who lives in the sewers.
N is for Nigel who likes to film tigers.
O is for Oscar who feels like a brick.
P is for Patrick who makes me feel sick.
Q is for Quentin who serves us all drinks.
R is for Ricky who looks like he stinks.
S is for Santa who always looks red.
T is for Tom who likes staying in bed.
U is for us when we like watching cartoons.
V is for Valerie who thinks people look like prunes.
W is for Warren who likes killing people loads.
X is for Xander who likes sending silly codes.
Y is for Yvonne who likes playing dirty tricks.
Z is for Zack who likes practising his kicks.

Charlotte Jakeman (9)
Northleigh CE Primary School

Brad's Poem

There once was a boy named Brad
Who was very lazy and sad
He was picking his nose
And goodness, who knows
What he would do if he was mad.

Bradley Morton (10)
Northleigh CE Primary School

The Flying Pig

Look, look, a flying pig
The one eating a fig
Stars and planets
Were titchy dots

Look, look, a fat pig
A fat, flying pig
He's whizzing, whizzing
Round the moon.

Look, look, a tall pig
A tall, fat, flying pig
What a funny sight
It's a flying pig

Look, look, a silly pig
A silly, tall, fat, flying pig
It's a big, flying pig.

Declan Amphlett (7)
Northleigh CE Primary School

Sports Day

S aturday is the day for sport,
P ole-vaulting, pole-vaulting is all I thought.
O r I'll think of the cross-country run,
R unning all around just for fun.
T iming me in 50 seconds flat,
S eeing Mum in a silly hat.

D rinking water, gulping it down,
A nd my baby brother has got a big frown.
Y ou'll see me here, only next year I'm going
                              to win all the races.

Stuart Puffett (10)
Northleigh CE Primary School

One Overgrown Tortoise

One overgrown tortoise sitting on a wall.
A hare came along and said . . .
'That's one big, ugly tortoise.'
Then a dog came along and barked . . .
'That's one big, fat and ugly tortoise.'
Then a cat came along and said . . .
'That's one big, fat, ugly and lazy tortoise.'
Then a rabbit came along and said . . .
'That's one big, fat, ugly, lazy and smelly tortoise.'
Then a frog came along and croaked . . .
'That's one big, fat, ugly, lazy, smelly and old tortoise.'
Then a snake came along and hissed . . .
'That's one big, fat, ugly, lazy, smelly, old and cranky tortoise.'
Then a fish came along and gurgled . . .
'Help, I can't breathe!'

Joe Brooker (9)
Northleigh CE Primary School

Growing Up

Great! I'm growing up!
Right now, I'm growing up?
Oh no! I'm growing up!
Why do I have to grow up?
I, am growing up?
No, I don't want to grow up!
Granny, how do you grow up?

Up, up, up, I'm growing up,
Please say twelve isn't growing up,
1, 2, 3, 4, 5, 6, 7, 8, 9, 10, 11, 12, 13,
14, 15, 16, 17, 18, 19, 20 and then there's
. . . *Oh no!*

Frances Purnell (10)
Northleigh CE Primary School

How Man U Won The Title

When Man U were playing Man City,
Man U were losing, what a pity.
Then they made a comeback,
Keane pulled 2 out of a hat.
Now they are champions, whoopee.

Later (the season after that),
Man U had to play Ajax.
Ronaldo got in a strop,
So he got sent off.
But the score was 4-0 (take that).

When Man U beat Juve,
The final was on the way.
They were against AC Milan,
They beat them (course they can),
Will they win it again some day?

Myles Cunningham (9)
Northleigh CE Primary School

Teachers From The Dump

Mr Dipstick wears lipstick
Mrs Fat ate a rat
Mr Tarzan loves marzipan
Mrs Bart wears jam tarts
Mr Stone eats a bone
Mr Williams owns billions!
Mrs Howells loves vowels
Mr Plug wears a rug and in the night he loves to hug
Mrs Die can fly
And that's the end of the *school of horror!*

Tom Milner (9)
Northleigh CE Primary School

TV And Mum

You're sitting there all day,
You're about to pay,
Mum is coming! Mum is coming!

You prepare yourselves for battle,
Perhaps I can hide behind the rattle,
Mum is coming! Mum is coming!

You hear the car coming, it fills you with dread,
It's driving you out of your head!
Mum is coming! Mum is coming!

You quickly run for the shed,
To get your bike named Ted,
Mum is coming! Mum is coming!

It's nearly midnight, I've got to think right,
I'm going to escape into the night,
Mum is coming! Mum is coming!

I can live with Ashley,
If he doesn't bash me,
Mum is coming! Mum is coming!

No, it's too late! The shed door falls down,
And in she comes, back from town,
Mum is here! Mum is here!

She rages in and throws me in the bin,
I think she wins,
Mum has won! Mum has won!

50 years without TV,
How can I live without the BBC,
Mum is horrid! Mum is horrid!

Next night . . . I'm filled with fear because,
A slap on the bum, why?
Mum is here! Mum is here!

Josh Williams (10)
Northleigh CE Primary School

The Grumpy Teacher

I walk in my classroom, I hear a shout.
I see that the grumpy teacher is up and about.
I open the door, she shouts in my ear.
'Get on with your work,' everyone can't hear.
It's assembly now, our teacher is jolly cross.
I think I'd rather go home in a bus.
I open my mouth, I give a big shout.

'Go home, everyone,' the bus is up and about.
I watch everyone disappear.
Then my teacher shouts clear in my ear.
Then she raises her voice.
Her fiery breath gives me no choice.
Just then I wake up in bed.
Oh, deary me, I've bashed my own head.

Fern Dawson (7)
Northleigh CE Primary School

Marsh-Mallow My Hamster!

Marsh-Mallow, Marsh-Mallow,
Where are you now?
You've eaten half the carpet,
Please come back to me now.
I'm searching, I'm searching,
But then I look.
You're back in your cage,
Snug as a bug.
And so pretty you look!

Matthew Green (9)
Northleigh CE Primary School

The Wind

I am the wind, the wandering wind,
The wind that rattles through Indian's huts,
Rocks the cradle, flickers the flame, swings the pot,
The same wind that blows the boughs, calms the angry ocean.
What will happen when the Indians are dead and gone?
Must I linger on?
No, I still swish around London streets,
Whisking people's hats away instead of huts.
I now try to enter things called houses,
Where doors are shut against me,
So I stay outside and howl,
The dogs begin to growl.
I whisper to the last trees in the world,
'Remember me in the name of your heavenly forefathers,
Remember, Brother Eagle, Sister Sky, remember.'

Rowan Whitehouse (8)
Northleigh CE Primary School

The Hedgehog

The hedgehog is a strange little creature,
Who rolls up in a ball,
He is very, very small but doesn't mind at all.
He can make himself very, very tense,
And does it all for his self-defence,
Even though he hibernates in a pile of leaves.
He's got many, many tricks up his prickly sleeves.
Now I have to say, 'Bye-bye,'
To catch my dinner of chicken pie.

Jamie MacKenzie (8)
Northleigh CE Primary School

Planets

The planets are wearing clothes,
Mercury is wearing bright red suits,
A comet flies past Venus,
And Earth wears blue and green.

Mars wears muddy brown,
And Saturn is covered in grey,
Jupiter puts on yellow, peach shirts,
And Neptune is covering itself in cream.

The last two planets are Uranus and Pluto,
And they are sky-blue and white,
Uranus is big and Pluto is small,
But they are the last of all.

Victoria Dexter (8)
Northleigh CE Primary School

The Crazy Animals

The cat's in the cupboard and the dog's on the loo,
The pigeon's in the attic and the donkey's stuck in glue,
The rabbit's playing hockey out on the street,
And the fox is by the fire warming up his feet.

The animals still wear nappies,
Which makes them very unhappy,
The hamster's in the garden, hanging up her clothes,
But down came an eagle and pecked off her nose.

The vet sees the hamster and takes her in a lorry,
I can tell you she's alive and that's the end of the story!

Philip Weatherill (9)
Northleigh CE Primary School

Kennings Owl

Night flier
Mouse seeker
Tree dweller
Loud screecher
Head turner
White feathered
Huge eyed
Powerful striker
Noble creature
Valiant bird
Day dreamer
Wisdom bringer
Bone flinger.

Jack Richards (10)
Northleigh CE Primary School

PC Finger Licker

PC Finger Licker licks everything in sight,
Once he even licked the wax of the candle-light.
He solves the crime by licking the floor,
Sometimes he licks my bedroom door.
He licks his finger, he licks his ear,
He licks everything far and near.
My mum thinks he's silly,
But I think he's cool, like my best friend, Billy.
One day, he licked a poisonous frog's head,
So poor old PC Finger Licker was . . . dead!

Rachel Martin (9)
Northleigh CE Primary School

Weather

People running in the street,
Trying to hide from all the sleet.
Sun is hot, we're playing out,
No need to whisper, just run and shout.
Oh no! Now it's pouring down,
Better go in or else we'll drown.
Snow comes downwards from the sky,
Let's go out, come on now, fly.
Wind is blowing through my hair,
Come on, let's run, I don't care.
Now come on, let's go sailing,
Don't be silly, it's just started hailing.

Alexandra Smith (9)
Northleigh CE Primary School

Dinosaur

Dinosaurs come in all shapes and sizes
From ugly to pretty.
Some are as tall as a man and
Some are as big as a house.
Some can eat you!
Some can't eat you.
Some can trample trees.
Some can only trample sticks.

Some are as long as a whale.
Some are as long as a car.

Jake Stromqvist (8)
Northleigh CE Primary School

People

A is for Andrew who stands on a ball
B is for Ben who fell off a brick wall
C is for Charlie who likes lots of chains
D is for Dan who likes to write names
E is for Eric who won't eat a carrot
F is for Freddie who has a pet parrot
G is for Garry who won't go to bed
H is for Harry who sleeps with a ted
I is for Izaac who likes to play rugby
J is for Joss who gives people a nuggy
K is for Kevin who won't stop to laugh
L is for Linda who likes to buy scarves
M is for Matt who has a big hat
N is for Nickie who has a huge bat
O is for Ollie who eats all his dinner
P is for Paris who thinks he's a winner
Q is for Queenie who has a big dog
R is for Roy who sits on the log
S is for Stuart who lives in a tree
T is for Troy who just hurt his knee
U is for Una who writes very neat
V is for Violet who likes to be beat
W is for Wren who likes to eat worms
X is for X-men who like to spread germs
Y is for Yvonne who has a big smile
Z is for Zoe who sleeps for a while.

Matthew Wren (9)
Northleigh CE Primary School

School Is Fun

We wear navy jumpers, our skirts and trousers are grey
We have quite a lot of play
School is fun
We like to run
They teach us how to add
Sometimes we are bad

We eat and eat and eat
Then we sit in our seat
My favourite subject is art
There's this horrid boy called Bart
Our teacher's always in a huff
Sometimes I'm out of puff

School is always fun
I feel I could run and run
Just to get to school
There isn't a swimming pool
But that's all right with me
I will be as quiet as can be.

Hannah Kenyon (9)
Northleigh CE Primary School

My Wild Teacher

My teacher is wild,
She swings around the classroom, she's wild.
My teacher roars so loud, I could swear she was a lion.
Charging like a rumping rhino through the plains of the classroom,
She treads on all the children with her large grey boots,
My teacher is wild.
'Ooah, ooah, sit down,' she screeches.
My friend says, 'She's probably half orang-utan and half baboon.'
But I don't think so, she's not orange and grey, but she's still wild.
My teacher is wild, she's a wild chick!

Jessica Smith (9)
Northleigh CE Primary School

It's Summer

It's summer,
and English clothes are changing,
the spring air has gone, the summer air is here,
and everyone's going to the beach,
playing with their beach balls, swimming in the sea,
children putting suncream on to make sure they don't get burnt,
splashing in the sea, being wrapped up warm in a towel,
and eating ice cream,
making some sandcastles, saying hi to everyone you know,
running up into the sand dunes, then running back down,
then going back home all wet and sandy.

Megan Hickling (9)
Northleigh CE Primary School

Rowing

Rowing down and down the river
Makes me jump and scream and shiver
Even though the boat is very safe
I know the water's deep
That's why rowing down the river
Makes me shiver.

Amy Straughan (9)
Northleigh CE Primary School

Flight Of The Hunting Kestrel

Airborne searcher,
Heartless hoverer,
Sharp spotter,
Meteoric descender,
Swift striker,
Rodent killer,
Motorway monster.

Nicholas Wilson (11)
Northleigh CE Primary School

It's Christmas!

It's Christmas,
And the houses are changing their themes,
Getting out trees with golden lights.
Putting up angels with glittering wings,
Having snow in your wolf-skin coat.
The bells dinging softly, as children laugh,
And sending out cards with holly and berries.
So at the end of the day you get tucked up in bed,
Waiting for Saint Nick to come once again.

Frankie Shackleton (9)
Northleigh CE Primary School

English

E nglish can be boring,
N obody knows everything about English!
G aining knowledge will always help,
L iteracy is clever in many ways.
I ndependent work is always better,
S o many names to remember!
H ow much work is there left to do?

Robert Derrington (10)
Northleigh CE Primary School

Horses

Prancing, galloping, trotting, racing,
All on a summer's day,
Dressage, fancy show and pacing,
They hardly make a snort or neigh,
With their owners up on their backs,
They go home, not to a ramshackle shack,
But to a stable warm and cosy,
But my favourite horse is called Rosy!

Vanessa Macdonald (9)
Northleigh CE Primary School

My Alphabet Poem Of Names

A is for Albert who is always late
B is for Bernese who never eats chocolate cake
C is for Chris who eats cheese nibbles
D is for Dan who has a cat called Tibbles
E is for Edna who loves scrambled eggs
F is for Freda who has some coat pegs
G is for Georgia who has a top hat
H is for Harry who has a gold tap
I is for Isabelle who sits around all day
J is for Josie who makes the weeks pay
K is for Kath who is very good at art
L is for Leon who likes jam tarts
M is for Michelle who has a big vest
N is for Natalie who has a big test
O is for Oliver who is a bit of a pain
P is for Peter who lives down the lane
Q is for Quentin who has a huge log
R is for Richard who has a coat with togs
S is for Sue who drinks orange juice
T is for Tony who is such a great use
U is for Una who sits on a chair
V is for Vicky and her teddy who make a great pair
W is for William who has a lump of gold
X is for Xavier who is very bold
Y is for Yvonne who eats lots of food
Z is for Zoe who has a huge mood.

Caryn Bristow (10)
Northleigh CE Primary School

My Dog Cinquain

My dog,
is young and black,
he digs in the garden,
he loves to run for a big bone,
to chew.

Cameron Heaton (8)
Northleigh CE Primary School

My Teacher

My teacher is very funny,
She drops everything,
And she's never ready when the basket girl comes.
In winter she wears her coat and scarf in doors,
She has brown hair and she doesn't have freckles.
Can you guess who she is?
She's Mrs Rowell.

Isabel Massey (9)
Northleigh CE Primary School

Autumn

Autumn's gone
Winter's come
Snow all around
All on the ground
Everywhere's cold
I've been told
Spring will come soon
Then summer as well
But summer is a long way away.

Pippa Lewis (9)
Northleigh CE Primary School

Tiger Cubs

T iger cubs are hard to manage.
I nteresting things like bugs are fun to watch.
G oing places with their mum.
E njoying all the days they have.
R unning about having fun.

C oming up to the car, seeing who is there.
U sing the car as a viewpoint.
B athing in the cool pond.
S ooner or later they'll grow older.

Abigail Smith (11)
Northleigh CE Primary School

Pirates

Pirates are so deadly, luckily they're dead
They all died with a bullet in the head
With a sword and a canon blasting everybody dead
They always chose a parrot as their talking pet
With a hook on their hand, knocking men off the plank
With a skull and crossbones being their flag
So they're kings of the sea, but not of the land
With a patch on their eye and a hat on their head
So now you see what pirates did before they were dead.

Charlie Bytheway (9)
Northleigh CE Primary School

Ponies' Day

P onies gallop everywhere.
O n and on they run.
N ow knowing where to run around the giant field.
I f you are weak with a pony it will do what it likes.
E very pony is sweet.
S ensible and sometimes naughty.

D irty little things they are, rolling in the mud.
A ny food they eat.
Y oung horses are so sweet, I wish I had one of my own.

Lucy Cooper (8)
Northleigh CE Primary School

Storm

Only clouds swirling round, round, round
Only rain dripping down, down, down
Only snow drifting softly, softly, softly
Only hail thundering loudly, loudly, loudly
Only thunder growling madly, madly, madly
Only a storm beating sadly, sadly, sadly.

Bethaney Allbright (11)
Northleigh CE Primary School

My Best Friend

(The best friend of this poem is Jo)

My friend Jo,
Is smaller than a bee,
As shy as the fishes,
As beautiful as can be.

As brainy as an owl,
As quick as lightning,
As hard as a nail,
As strong as an ox.

As soft as a teddy,
As silly as a sausage,
As sleepy as you and me,
As messy as a pig.

The friend of this poem,
Will never tell lies,
But goes hyper once in a while,
(Or so I say).

Grace Harker (11)
St Nicholas CE Middle School, Pinvin

Teacher's Weather Forecast

Miss Fluorescent-blue will be shining bright all day,
But now and then she'll hit a cloud, then you'll have to move out
the way.

Mr Green will be very misty and nothing will be seen,
But then he'll brightly shine, but watch out, he may not be kind.

Mrs Black will be rushing down the corridor, with thunderstorms
of rage,
Then she'll turn really mean, with lightning striking again.

Mr Red will be shining so bright with happiness, he might explode,
Then he'll hit some hail, which will really change his mode.

Joanna Train (10)
St Nicholas CE Middle School, Pinvin

Freddy's Big Bump

It's such a shame,
It's such a shame,
What happened to awful Freddy.
He walked alone from Polypolone,
And fell and bumped his heady.
His mum had a note to say 'What happened?'
'We do not know,' it said.
But some say they heard him crying when he was
Falling
And
Dying
Then
Dead!

Alec Smith (10)
St Nicholas CE Middle School, Pinvin

Billy The Broom

I'm Billy the broom
My job is sweeping the dust
I sweep and sweep from room to room
Cleaning is a must

From carpets to tiles
I clean and sweep
It seems like miles and miles
Even upstairs I creep

Outside I brush up the leaves
Off the lawn and drive
Bags of rubbish my master heaves
It's great to be alive

My day is done
I've finished my work
All the rubbish is gone
Now I'm going back to bed where spiders lurk.

Alice Nicklin (10)
St Nicholas CE Middle School, Pinvin

Me!

(Based on 'The Writer Of This Poem' by Roger McGough)

The writer of this poem
Is as quick as a thrust SSC
He is smaller than a mouse
And as happy as can be.

As complicated as a microchip
As simple as a cow
As boring as a mop
As exciting as a 'Wow!'

As tricky as a piece of string
As fiddly as a vine
As useful as a pair of wings
As fun as drinking wine!

Who's as evil as a devil
As dangerous as killer bees
As wiggly as a vine weevil
The answer: Me!

Sebastian Shaw (11)
St Nicholas CE Middle School, Pinvin

Slickuterene

I'm sticky, I'm mean,
I'm slickuterene,

I stick here and there,
And everywhere!

I can stick on your wall,
And I won't fall.

Everyone can wear me with pride and joy,
Every little girl and boy,

I'm slick, slick
Slickuterene!

Sophie Edwards (10)
St Nicholas CE Middle School, Pinvin

The Teacher Forecast

Mrs Francis
Will be thunder and lightning at times but the
Rest of the day sunny spells.

Miss Smith
Will be sunny spells throughout the whole day
With some bursts of rage.

Mrs Rix
Will be sunny spells with some heavy showers
At times.

Mrs Chatterton
Will be bright throughout the day with some
Outbreaks of rage after dinner time.

Mr Kelly
Will be bursting with rage throughout the day
So watch out kids, it's gonna get messy.

Ryan Perks (10)
St Nicholas CE Middle School, Pinvin

Car Keys

Where are my car keys? Where have they gone?
I've got to find them, I can't take long,
Last I had them they were near the car,
I've got to find them, they can't be far.

Keep looking and looking, are they up in a tree?
Keep looking and looking and make sure you hurry,
We've got to find them, are they in the flat?
We've got to find them, are they under a mat?

Keep looking and find them and hurry up,
Keep looking and find them, are they in a cup?
Make sure they're not still in their socket,
Upsy daisy, they're in my pocket!

Charlotte Ruff (10)
St Nicholas CE Middle School, Pinvin

Rugby

When I go to a match
I play a bit of catch
We love it when we win
We hate it when we lose
But when we do win
The adults go for some booze.

Beginning of the match
I put on my rugby kit
Then I say we're going to win it
I practice a bit of catch
Then it's time to go and play the match.

Half-time
If we are losing, the adults can't go boozing,
If we are winning, we're just standing and sitting.

End of the match
If we have won
We're just having lots of fun
If we just lose
The adults go home without their booze.

Josh Sutterby (11)
St Nicholas CE Middle School, Pinvin

What Do Teachers Do After Half-Past Three?

What do teachers do after half-past three?
Do they just sit there all night drinking endless cups of tea?

Do they create evil tests
And read them through with zest?

Do they just sit in their classroom and watch telly all night
Or mark test papers, making sure the answers are right?

What they do we will never know,
If they stay at school or just go,
It really is a mystery,
What teachers do after half-past three!

Francesca Gordon (10)
St Nicholas CE Middle School, Pinvin

Snap Attack!

Old Mrs Mime was on the toilet,
Doing what people do,
Everything was perfect,
Until a shark dived out the loo.

Now you'll probably want to know
What happened to Mrs Mime,
If you really want to hear the truth
She didn't get off in time.

But Mrs Mime was a wrestler
In her early life,
All her fans nicknamed her,
The Dagger and the Knife.

Remembering all her moves
She swung some deadly kicks
She killed the shark and it proves
Sharks and old ladies don't mix.

She was rather hungry
She thought she would boil it
But in the end she decided
She'd flush it back down the toilet!

Fred Simmons (10)
St Nicholas CE Middle School, Pinvin

Mountains

I am a mountain, rough and tall,
My echo sounds like a lonely call,
The tops of me are covered in snow,
When you're on the floor, you're really low,
When you're at the top, you're really high,
In the clouds and in the sky,
People go up in a cable car
To see a beautiful stunning art.
So go for yourself, take a look
I promise you, you won't need a book.

Jessica Morris (11)
St Nicholas CE Middle School, Pinvin

The Teacher Weather Forecast

Good morning and welcome to the teacher's forecast

Miss Smith will be bright and cheerful in the morning
but beware her mood will change in the afternoon.
Mrs Chatterton will be gloomy when she finds she has a cold
when her nose is as red as a tomato.
Mr Kelly will be raining strictness so do not annoy him
today until 12.15pm.
Mrs Rix will be in a shower of sun, but screaming snow
when she sits on a wasp in her room.
Mr Dawes will be in a sunny spot, but will change suddenly
so beware of the rage.
Mrs Saddington will be bright and breezy even if the
weather's dull and cloudy.
Mr Furber will be cold as snow in the morning and very
hot by the end of the day.

Thank you for listening to the teacher's weather forecast.
Have a good day.

Rebecca Lear (10)
St Nicholas CE Middle School, Pinvin

Weather On Monday

Watch out there will be hail while Mr Kelly teaches 6a,
Miss Smith will be sunshine with a few showers,
Mrs Rix with rain and a bit of snow,
Now I'm sure the kids are in for sunshine,
Lily should have an outburst of lightning at -5,
Ellie will have snow throughout the afternoon at 0,
Hayden will have sunshine with drizzles of rain at 10,
Melanie will be raining with an overcast sky,
By the time Sam reaches room 13, there will be a hurricane,
Katie will have clear skies, so you can go bird watching,
Some drizzle around Tom as he has a cold,
It's going to be teeth chatteringly cold around Mrs Chatterton,
It could be north or south winds for Mrs Chalk,
All in all, it's going to be a stormy day for the children of 6a.

Hannah Downs (11)
St Nicholas CE Middle School, Pinvin

Fire

I can burn you to ashes,
In a one, two, three,
No one's more powerful,
More powerful than me!
I'm as little as a servant,
But as big as a master,
When I get you, you'll need more than a plaster,
You'll be ashes in a click,
And as dead as a dodo.
I've killed everyone else,
So you're now solo,
I will burn you to death,
And you will die,
I'll burn everything,
To the very last fly,
I have no weakness,
So I am strong,
What, you have water?
I can hear my funeral bells ring.

I'm dying, I'm dead,
Bells go ding.

Thomas Neal (10)
St Nicholas CE Middle School, Pinvin

My Little Brother

My little brother is a big, big pain
He's been like it since he tripped over a drain,
Sometimes he acts like my big sister
And sometimes he acts like a big fat twister,
He hates fish fingers, baked beans and stew,
He says if he eats it, he will need the loo,
His name is Lawrence not Lawrece
If anybody calls him it, he'll tie himself up in a fleece,
I'm afraid I'll have to draw this to a close
Because my brother's got a runny nose!

Rebecca East (10)
St Nicholas CE Middle School, Pinvin

Time For A Change

What's that smell?
I don't feel well,
Mum!
Change the baby,
I don't mean maybe,
Please change his nappy
And make us happy,
He's all poopy,
The nappy's all gloopey,
Get the wet wipes,
Wipe him all clean,
Now a shiny bum can be seen,
Dry and clean and sweet,
What's that smell?
Oh, that's his feet!

Lily Barrett (10)
St Nicholas CE Middle School, Pinvin

Age

When you're young
You're naughty and bad,
Scream at Mum
And kick Dad.

When you're an adult,
You think you're cool,
Put on your heels,
And fall in the pool.

When you're old,
You think you're sweet,
Take off your shoes
And smell your feet.

Lara Smith (9)
St Nicholas CE Middle School, Pinvin

Bald Eagle

I can soar through the air
At miraculous speed,

And when I am hungry
I swoop down to feed,

I can perch on a tree
And look for my prey.

But I can go without food
For day after day.

I hunt for small creatures
And rabbits too

I would really laugh
If one of them flew!

Have you guessed who I am yet?
Take one last look.

I'm a bald eagle,
Way better than any old rook!

Victoria Woolley (11)
St Nicholas CE Middle School, Pinvin

Sam's Poem

As Mummy and Steve make their vows of love
Before all who came from near and far,
To show they care,
This day is filled with happiness,
A joy, that is all ours to share.

The prayer we carry in our hearts,
Of love and faith and peace,
We give to you with every hope,
That these will never cease.

Sam Evan White-Edwards (10)
St Nicholas CE Middle School, Pinvin

That's My Sister, Rebecca

My sister is a pain,
She always ruins our favourite game
And always gets the blame,
That's my sister, Rebecca.

My sister's sometimes fun,
When her dirty deed is done,
She is great to play with,
That's my sister, Rebecca.

My sister's often helpful,
Although she can be doubtful,
She helps around the house,
That's my sister, Rebecca.

My sister's often kind,
So I think that you will find,
She can be very thoughtful,
That's my sister, Rebecca.

Jessica Smith (10)
St Nicholas CE Middle School, Pinvin

Blood

Dripping blood in the night,
Drip, drip, drip,
An evil shadow stretching across the room,
Sitting in bed, in pain
Drinking tea and biscuits being dipped.

People visiting here and there,

Bustling around, I don't really care,
Blood still dripping,
I'm not hungry,
Blood fading out of me - help!

Millie Boddy (10)
St Nicholas CE Middle School, Pinvin

The Eagle Of Doom

Eyes as red as oozing blood,
Wings as strong as rhinos,
Beak as sharp as a fighting dagger,
Much more than a roaring lion.

Don't look into its piercing eyes,
They will stun you for ten years,
But the terrifying warning is,
Beware of the eye hidden in its wings.

If it spies something good,
It will open with a crack,
And then you'll know what's in for you,
Stunned for evermore.

Lucy Hanson (10)
St Nicholas CE Middle School, Pinvin

Sam My Dog

I have a big black Labrador,
That means everything to me,
He may be old and he can be a pain,
But he fills me up with glee.

My dog is a pain,
Because he always runs away,
And one time he ran away and I could not find him,
But he came back straight away, hooray!

I have a big black Labrador,
That means everything to me,
Yes he may be old and yes he can be a pain,
But he still fills me with glee.

Lucy Taylor (9)
St Nicholas CE Middle School, Pinvin

My Imaginary Friend

My imaginary friend
Is always going round the bend.
Up and down, round and round,
I'm surprised she doesn't make a sound.

When my friend is playing with me,
She always comes in to see.
So I tell her to go away
And come again another day.

But I hear her singing quietly,
'Mary, Mary quite contrary . . .'
But I must be dreaming
Because she is only imaginary.

Rachel Corbett (10)
St Nicholas CE Middle School, Pinvin

Red Ruby

A red and shiny ruby
Which has just been dug out of the ground,
Been placed in a museum,
To stay overnight.

The horrid little ruby
Melted the glass down,
Rolled right out of the cushion
And tripped all of the way down to town.

It came and twirled and whirled,
Down and down and down,
The hip hop splash,
It went in a flash,
But no longer was it seen.

Katie Hickinbotham (10)
St Nicholas CE Middle School, Pinvin

In My Magic Box

(Based on 'Magic Box' by Kit Wright)

In my magic box I would have
A lovely bar of milk chocolate
With a packet of Coke bottles next to it.

The picture of my Jack Russell, Monty
When he was a puppy.

A teeny baby rabbit ready to jump out of its pen.

Also a hot, lush swimming pool, ready to jump in.

My best blue and purple cuddly toy called Twizzels.

And my lovely, modern, comfy bedroom
With all my toys in it.

Jessica Hawthorn (9)
St Nicholas CE Middle School, Pinvin

My Magic Box

(Based on 'Magic Box' by Kit Wright)

In my magic box I would find my family
Because they are very special to me and
Because they are always there for me.

I would also have my bed when it is warm,
Comfortable and cosy with all my soft toys
Gathered all around it.

I would also have all of my friends because they are all kind.
I would put in Felicity, Paige,
Chloe, Olivia, Eleanor and Rosy.

I would have Mrs Hooper
When she is really happy and smiling.

Diane Barker (9)
St Nicholas CE Middle School, Pinvin

Sauron Out Of Lord Of The Rings

His big red eyes like the blazing sun,
Searching for the ring of power, this must be done.
He shall kill anything in his path,
He is searching through dirt and green, soft grass.

He stamps here and there with his bulky feet,
But the ring of power still he must seek.
His helmet disguises his face,
He is destroying this wondrous place.

Smashing houses, killing people,
Does he know the selfish Sméagol?
Living in Mordor with full deceit
Should he give Uruk-hai their release?

The ring is getting closer to Mount Doom,
The evil spread will go soon.
Frodo holds it over the pit of fire,
Anyone who falls in will burn inside her.

He drops the ring and evil goes,
Now this book should be closed.

Hector Davies (10)
St Nicholas CE Middle School, Pinvin

The Ice Cream

The ice cream is waiting to be licked,
He is melting very fast,
But the tongue gets nearer;
Nearer and nearer.

And then he is licked,
The flake so delicious,
The tenderness filling the eater's mouth,
And then he is gone.

Eleanor Britton (10)
St Nicholas CE Middle School, Pinvin

Ali

Ali thinks he is an angel,
As weird as they come.
He scares his little teddy,
And upsets his little tum!

One morning in November,
They took him to the park.
He jumped off a slide,
Because he thought it was an ark.

He got ever so dirty,
He got ever so messy.
He went a mile to his next-door neighbour,
And he got his friend called Bessie.

Now Ali knows he is a devil,
He's got a mummy's curse.
At night he is a werewolf,
But his brother's even worse.

Alasdair McGillivray (10)
St Nicholas CE Middle School, Pinvin

The Thunder In The Sky

The cracking thunder
In the jet-black midnight sky,
Scaring those children
And their mothers desperately.

The mothers in their beds
Desperately trying to ignore
The screams of their children,
The calling of their young ones
Upsets the baby
In its soft, high-sided cot.

Olivia A Wiles (9)
St Nicholas CE Middle School, Pinvin

Tash

My dog is called Tash,
She's got a sash,
She jumps around,
Without making a sound.

She kills her toys,
And really likes boys,
She licks her spoon
And howls in tune.

When she goes dog training,
She keeps swinging and swaying.
We put her on a lead
To cut down her speed.

When she's in the playroom,
She lobs her Father Christmas across the room,
She whacks and whacks and whacks
Her special friend called Max.
When she's down the lane,
She's a big pain,
She tugs and tugs on her lead,
She digs and digs to pull up a weed.

Jaeren Coathup (9)
St Nicholas CE Middle School, Pinvin

The Man Who Can See Time

I am Saruman and I can see time
But I can't see Celador's hair that burns in the sky.
Where is the herald, the herald of the ring?
That ring is more to me than Frodo Baggins could ever dream.
I will send an army to fight in my stead,
But will my army find the ring?
Maybe, maybe not, but the battle will never end.

Myles Weaver (9)
St Nicholas CE Middle School, Pinvin

My Magic Box

(Based on 'Magic Box' by Kit Wright)

In my magic box I would have
My cosy, warm and relaxing bed.

I would also have refreshing
Blanket that comforts me
Whenever I need it.

I would also have all the love
That my mum, dad and
My two brothers give me.

I would also have all of my treasured
Family because they care for me and
Look after me every day.

I would also have my fluffy, soft and cute kittens.

Felicity Parkinson-Allsopp (9)
St Nicholas CE Middle School, Pinvin

The Terrible Trip

One morning on a school day, our school went on a trip,
A boy was eating an apple. *Whoops!* He swallowed a pip.
A girl came in and saw him, she said, 'What have you done?'
'I swallowed a pip,' he said, 'can I have your plum?'

'Hello!' said the teacher on the school bus,
A boy saw an eagle and made such a fuss.
'Right, off we go,' said Mrs Allo.
'Can I go to the toilet, Miss?'
'Go and ask Miss Flo.'

'Miss, I need the toilet, please Miss, please,'
'All right then, go on then, go, go go, go, go.'
'Why did you eat the peas then?'
'I don't know, know, know.'

Olivia Hartley (9)
St Nicholas CE Middle School, Pinvin

Skateboarding Mayhem

S oaring through the air,
K ick flips most of the way,
A cid drops of big blocks,
T ail grabs up a half-pipe,
E lisa Steamer is a pro,
B am Magara go!
O llie's everywhere,
A irwalks all the time.
R amps curved, ramps straight, ramps that you can skate.
D eath could come if you bail a big!
I ndys happening up ramps,
N ose stalls everywhere,
G rinding on poles, then you fall off and land with a crack at the neck.

Joshua Lawton (9)
St Nicholas CE Middle School, Pinvin

Lord Of The Rings

L ord Sauron, lord of all evil,
O ne ring to bind them all together.
R ing of power to cover all the land in darkness,
D efenders of Minas Tirith.

O rc - the army of Mordor,
F ellowship to protect Frodo.

T reachery of Isenguard
H obbits that destroyed the rings.
E vil that lingers in the darkness.

R ights of passage,
I ntelligence of the riders of Rohan,
N eedless Gollum,
G andalf the white
S aving all.

Luke Sephton (10)
St Nicholas CE Middle School, Pinvin

5h

Ellie is annoying,
Jessica is loud,
Lucy is quiet,
Mrs Hooper is proud!

Harry is brainy,
Jamie should be in a zoo,
Steph is the new girl,
Ben always needs the loo.

Luke likes tae kwon do,
Ed is cool,
Lucy H likes cheetahs,
Andy will always rule!

Josh is always naughty,
Felicity is pretty,
Josh is forgetful,
Jarren has a kitty!

Jess is always working,
Alex has a gun,
Olivia W is bossy,
Olivia H is fun!

Jessica Sykes (10)
St Nicholas CE Middle School, Pinvin

My Family

Bubbles in the bathroom,
Mud in the house,
When Mum sees this,
She's going to shout,
'Get the cat out,
He's making muddy puddles.'
Dad's locked the dog in the garden shed,
Everything is mad
And Mum's gone red.

Steph McStay (10)
St Nicholas CE Middle School, Pinvin

My Dream

Last night I had a great dream
And this is how it goes:

The sky was blue,
The sand was soft,
The sea was calm.

The sun was warm,
The seagulls were flying so high,
It was a perfect day.

In the distance I could hear a sound,
As I listened I knew it was my favourite group,
I could hardly believe my ears.

Before I knew it I was on stage dancing with the band,
The applause was loud and the cheers were too,
Then I realized it was all on TV.

I had only fallen asleep on the sofa at home!

Jo Gaze (10)
St Nicholas CE Middle School, Pinvin

The Three Little Pigs

Once there were three little pigs,
For all I know they all wore wigs.

They moved into a house of their own,
As far as I know they all had phones.

Along came a wolf that said, 'Hello,'
The pigs said, 'Go away or you'll blow.'

Away he went and blow he did,
The pigs ran away and surely hid.

They never came back,
And the wolf fell down with a clackety-clack.

Abigail Pallett (9)
St Nicholas CE Middle School, Pinvin

The Pets

Chris has 2 guinea pigs,
They are hard to catch,
They run around the garden,
And run away from Chris.

I have a gerbil,
He likes his ball,
He makes me look a fool.
He's hard to catch,
He's fast and he's small.

But the dog is big,
And he acts cool.
He likes it under the table,
He sleeps on the chair.

He likes his dad,
He plays with the ball,
They're the pets -
They are all cool.

Daniel Spencer (9)
St Nicholas CE Middle School, Pinvin

Cheeky Monkey

I know a cheeky monkey
Who lives on my front doorstep
He has got a funny name
And that funny name is Pep.

He is also very cheeky
Just like a little monkey
He likes to eat bananas
And he thinks he is quite funky.

I really like my monkey
Who is my favourite pet
There is something he really hates
That has to be the vet.

Abigail Jones (10)
St Nicholas CE Middle School, Pinvin

Suzan's Day

Wake up Suzan get out of bed
because you have a big day ahead.
Make your bed, shake your head,
and get ready for a big day.

Eat your breakfast really fast,
or you will be the last.
Go out of the door
before I say 'Or,'
Don't miss the bus or I'll go mad
and you'll have to deal with your dad.

Do your lessons, eat your lunch,
then it's out to play with the usual bunch.
Off we go, run, hop and skip,
the games we play are very hip.

We go inside, have a good read,
it's science next, we're planting seeds,
then come home, have your tea
and go and see Uncle Lee.

Then it's time for Suzan to go to bed
and relax her very poor head.

Kelly Ryder (10)
St Nicholas CE Middle School, Pinvin

The Ring

There once was a young hobbit,
He found a solid gold ring,
He had a sword called Sting.
He killed a whacking great spider,
He rode a barrel to Lake Town,
Then he went to find Smaug.

Josh Critchley (10)
St Nicholas CE Middle School, Pinvin

Time

Swooping, swirling, moving, hurling,
Such is the course of time.

Zooming, howling, screaming, showering,
Such is the way of time.

Life, death, movement, breath,
Such is the choice of time.

Lust, greed, power, breed,
Such is the way of man.

Always trying, trying to catch it, always trying, trying to get a bit,
Such are the thoughts of man.

Science is in its prime, trying to take power from time.
Such is what man can do.

Harry Mallinson (10)
St Nicholas CE Middle School, Pinvin

Parents

My mum is super,
But I don't know how she copes.
She has to live with us kids,
And she doesn't have a hope!

My dad is brill,
But I don't know how he copes.
He has to live with us kids
And he doesn't have a hope!

But when they're together,
They're as good as can be,
Coping with my brother
And coping with me!

Ellie Morris (9)
St Nicholas CE Middle School, Pinvin

My Class

Liam Avery likes acting and telling jokes,
Luke Barnett is very quiet and sensible too,
Kate Burman is a good friend and as quiet as can be,
Sam Cave has neat handwriting and likes to doodle,
Rebecca Dawkes is very brainy and is in set 1 maths,
Rebecca Gillmore likes daydreaming whilst playing with her hair,
Max Griffiths is sensible and sits by Luke in class.

Grace Harker is my best friend like all the people I know,
Eleanor Heath works hard and is very helpful,
I (Megan Heeks) think I'm very helpful.
Laura Higgins is one of my friends, she is very trustworthy,
Sarah Hutchings is quiet and friendly,
Alex Irish sometimes daydreams and he talks a lot,
Abigail Jones likes to laugh at a lot of things.

Nathan Jones is very funny and is very noisy,
Joe Kacarevic is also noisy and a bit weird,
Jack Mason is as noisy as noisy can be,
Adam Mobbs is very noisy, his nickname is Patch,
Andrew Price is brainy definitely in English,
Charlotte Ruff is funny and she is really fit,
Michael Savage likes science and is also brainy.

Lauren Smith is just like Charlotte but not as fit,
William Smith is very brainy and a little bit funny,
Dan Teasdale is very funny and is always talking,
Larissa Turvey is new to my class and is quiet.

Nick Tyler is funny and likes loads of things,
Ben Warren is funny and good at drawing,
Alex Woodman is a good friend and is funny,
Mrs Rix is a great teacher and is funny.

That's all of us in 6R and we work as a *team*.
We are the 6R *team*.

Megan Heeks (11)
St Nicholas CE Middle School, Pinvin

Good Morning This Is The Friend Forecast

Georgie Worthington

She will be happy and joyful for the day.
And after school when she is at the park
She will be sunny and jolly as well.

Emma Hawtree

She will be sunny and happy.
But she will still be quiet as usual.

Jo Williams

She will be lively and bouncy and will also be playful and jolly.
But she might be upset for some of the day.

Jojo Train

She will be happy and will do well in lessons.
She will be heading for clear sunshine.

Jo Gaze

She will be heading for storms.
Maybe even thunder and lightning.

Sophia Richards

She will be heading for rainy weather,
But will clear up in the afternoon.

Georgie Bailey (10)
St Nicholas CE Middle School, Pinvin

The Tiger

The tiger has wise eyes,
He knows about men,
They put traps to kill him.
They will take his coat
For rich ladies to wear.
The tiger is angry.
So am I!

Chris Billingham (10)
St Nicholas CE Middle School, Pinvin

The Lion And The Tiger

The lion and the tiger
went to space
in a beautiful violin case.

They took some lamb
and plenty of ham,
tied up in a red shoelace.

Loud sang the lion
and the tiger joined in,
and the tiger he played
a pink violin.
And lo and behold,
they found a bread mould,
and found out that they were in a bin.

'Oh dear,' said the lion, 'that was such a waste.'
'Oh dear!' screamed the tiger, 'I thought we were in space.'
So out of the bin they climbed,
and saw many stars,
looked left, right and down
and saw that they were on Mars.

Christopher Butcher-Calderón & James Michael Smith (10)
Stanley Road Primary School

Please Dad!

P lease Daddy, can I sit in your chair?
E asy life is in your chair.
A ll around me peaceful in your chair,
C omfy, cosy chair,
E ating chocolate in your chair . . . Daddy!

Lucy Hencher
Stanley Road Primary School

My Dad's On The Transfer List

On offer,
One funny 34-year-old taxi driver,
Is good at jokes,
But some aren't funny,
Kind and smiley,
But he hates to get dirty,
Guaranteed to break things twice a day,
730 times (normal year)
732 times (leap year).
Tries to be clever
But . . . fails!
He asks for tea 3 times a day
1095 times (normal year)
1098 times (leap year)
Sadly lazy,
Plus daydreams,
Snores aloud through the night.
Only £5.55.
Any takers?
(I'll have him back in the summer!)

Aumair Qayum (10)
Stanley Road Primary School

Peace

P eace
E ats noises
A ll the time through the
C entre and out so it becomes quiet
E xcept for a drop of sound.

Amy Bull (11)
Stanley Road Primary School

The Titanic

I thought I heard a rumble,
I took a look outside.
A screaming lady rushing past, cried,
'The ship is going to capsize!'

'But the great Titanic is unsinkable,'
Or so that's what they said,
And when it hit an iceberg,
They cried, 'Stop worrying, don't lose your head.'

I suddenly heard a groaning,
The ship was being ripped apart.
I rushed upstairs to the very top deck,
And felt throbbing in my heart.

The mothers and children cried,
As they left the men on board.
The lifeboats now were being lowered,
As up in the air, flares soared.

I leapt onto a lifeboat,
One of the last who did leave,
Then an almighty crack echoed in the air,
And the ship began to heave.

I watched from the lifeboat in horror,
As the Titanic began to split.
One half sank deeper and deeper,
As the other started to lift.

The great ship was gone in minutes,
Vanishing beneath the waves.
We sailed around in our little boats,
To see how many people we'd save.

Ryan Sanders-Fox (11)
The Mount School

The Dolphin

I step into the water,
My head begins to swim,
And then this creature looks at me and smiles.
I smile back,
I am told to put my arms on his back and fin,
Then my beautiful dolphin looks at me and smiles.
I smile back.
He moves so swiftly
And his skin is so smooth,
He is a beautiful silver and blue and I love him.
Then he looks at me and smiles,
And I smile back
As he shakes his fin and says farewell.

Hannah Duffey (10)
The Mount School

The Soldier

The soldier got blown to the floor,
He saw his arm a metre away from his body.
He knew this was the end!
His face was covered in mud,
He felt himself being lifted,
Then he was carried to a bed,
He was in terrible pain.
He could hear the sound of shouting and screaming
And the banging of bombs.
He thought it would never end,
Then it all went black and he died.

Then the war ended
And he was just a memory.

Jack Newman (10)
The Mount School

The Crook

Crash goes the window,
He comes in.
The crook steals,
Steals lots of things . . .

He steals jewellery, expensive plates and money,
He looks upstairs and
Trashes the cupboards.
Steals our clothes,
Sprints down the stairs,
Takes the keys,
Smashes the window,
Jumps in the car
And shoots away.

We're left alone
All sad and depressed,
Now we're cleaning up the mess.

James Higginbottom (10)
The Mount School

The Snowstorm

The white, soft, silky snow
Darting this way and that,
While the rooftops shine in white.

In the far distance are the bare snow-covered trees,
The roads are all white and sparkling,
More and more snowflakes come down every second.
Now there is ice on the roads . . .
Cars are sliding this way and that.

The white, soft, silky snow . . .
Hides danger!

Jack Sims (11)
The Mount School

War

First the First World War,
Next the Second World War,
Then the Panama War,
And the Falklands War,
And, finally, the Gulf War.
Hooray! War is over.
Let us remember the people who died in those wars.

But . . . war is not over . . .
The Iraq War!
Americans go over to Iraq to try to stop Saddam,
But we are still in Iraq today.

There is still a man from the Gulf War suffering . . .
His legs in a bloodbath,
He used to have a shiny eye, now it is black,
A broken arm,
He waits till death comes,
But it never does,
So he keeps on suffering.

Nobody knows how many wars there will be in the future.

Ryan Hughes (10)
The Mount School

Space

In space there are planets and stars,
Lovely to see, lovely to watch.
Beautiful stars especially the golden sun,
And our moon that shines in the night,
Making us feel happy,
I love planets and their multicolours,
I love finding out about them at space centres.
I love looking up at all the planets around me.
I really like space.

Kyle Ashworth (9)
The Mount School

Animals - Great And Small

The ant, as tiny as a pinhead,
I see as I look to the ground.
The mouse squeaking under the floorboards,
I hear in my house.
The cat, furry and soft,
Happy and playful.
The dog, obedient to its master,
Good at keeping itself safe.
The horse, fast and stylish,
With a glossy coat.
The massive elephant, superior, big and strong,
Could knock a man down with its mighty tusks.
The giraffe, tall and graceful
Walking around in safari.
The human . . . the most destructive animal of all.

These animals could die because of us.

Dominic Denton (10)
The Mount School

The Mysterious Horse

The hooves that clatter on the ground,
The mane and tail that swish in the force of the wind.
The silver moon makes everything come alive,
And makes things change as well.
The galloping horse changes from black to white,
And finds a stream to drink from.
The sun comes up,
The moon goes down,
But there's no horse you can see,
Not even a shadow of that horse.
All you can hear are hooves and the sounds of slurps of water,
As the mysterious horse disappears . . .

Stephanie Hosking (10)
The Mount School

The Universe

The stars glisten and twinkle in the universe,
The big round planets are covered by mist.
Some planets are blue, some are red,
The big, wide, dark universe is cold and silent.
Meteors hurtling through space,
Colours are swirling,
Space is a marvel.

Oliver Hughes-Clarke (9)
The Mount School

Fireworks

Fireworks, fireworks,
The wonderful sound
Of them sizzling in the air.
Wonderful colours, red, greens and yellows,
Who could imagine the wonderful colours and noise
Of the fun, and the laughing and sounds?

Ashley Downes (9)
The Mount School

Rainbow

How would you like to ride on a rainbow,
Beautiful colours with beautiful light?

Indigo and violet,
Orange, red and blue,
Seven shining colours,
Green and yellow too.

Then if I'm lucky,
Or so I've been told,
Right at the end
Is my own pot of gold.

Charlotte Roden (9)
The Mount School

The Creation

I created the light,
I created the dark,
I created the sky,
And in it the lark.

I created the land,
Hills, rivers and seas,
Things to grow on the Earth,
Plants, flowers and trees.

I made the sun,
Moon and stars,
I made planets,
Pluto, Venus and Mars.

I made animals,
Then the days,
After I made people,
People to do my ways.

I was happy with this,
With the Earth I had made,
I wanted rest,
The Earth started to fade.

I woke in the morning,
Adam and Eve looked at me,
I ordered something,
I said, 'Do not touch that tree!'

The Devil came to Eve,
He said to eat the fruit,
She felt small,
She even felt minute.

Eve ate the fruit,
She gave some to Adam,
(Eve started to wonder)
Now what will happen?

I came back to the garden,
Adam and Eve hid away,
I walked towards them,
It was to their dismay.

I sent them right away,
I sent them right out,
They didn't come back,
(That's without a doubt!)

That was the start of the creation,
But not of the world that was made,
Now we say thank you to God,
Because he didn't kill us, *he saved!*

Bethan Winter (9)
The Mount School

Snow

Gently drifting on the wind,
The snow so mild and yet so cold.
Not a noise disturbs the winter air.

Down the snow comes, not a care in the world,
The wind on its back,
Softly it floats.

The sun is hiding
Behind a cloud,
Giving a little glimmer to the world.

The whole world is shining,
Full of cool, white snow,
What a dream it is,
The whole world a giant cake,
Snow as icing.

So cold.

Robert Lee (10)
The Mount School

Snowflakes

Snowflakes here! Snowflakes there!
Snowflakes now are everywhere.
Landing softly on the ground,
Spinning, twirling all around.
Toppling, twisting without a sound.

Snowflake, snowflake high up there,
Twisting, turning here and there,
Flying, flipping around and around
Into the sunset safe and sound.

William Tresidder (8)
The Mount School

Nelly

There was a cute little girl called Nelly
Who went out instead of watching the telly,
She fell in a pond, very gungy and smelly,
And got soaked right up to her belly.

Jack Pendlebury (9)
The Mount School

Hallowe'en

In the middle of the night on Hallowe'en
Ghosts, bats and vampires come to life
Children dress as witches, ghouls and ghosts
Ready for trick or treat

They knock on your door and say, 'Boo!'
Old people are scared
They sometimes scream and shout, 'Go away!'

When the sun sets
Ghosts, vampires and witches will come to life
On the next Hallowe'en night.

Ga Kei Sin (9)
The Mount School

The Wind

I am the wind,
The powerful wind.
People don't see me,
Yet they hear me.
People don't smell me
But they feel me.
I slither, I'm quick,
I can take you off your feet,
I can be destructive or calm
And can do some harm.
I knock on the door
And blow you away.
I rattle the windows
Until another day.

Alhasan Alhabib (9)
The Mount School

Untitled

I am the goalie,
I play for my school,
I feel excited,
I feel a bit scared as I go to the goalposts,
A whistle blows,
The ball is passed,
They're coming towards me,
I put my arms out wide,
I leap for the ball,
Mostly I get it,
I throw it to my team,
And I feel safe once again.

Lloyd Raybone (10)
The Mount School

My Feelings

I am a tree, big and bold,
But my leaves are tumbling away,
I feel my trunk will fall over
As my big branches sway.

But then I feel raindrops
It has started like that,
What shall I do? It's cold and wet,
As I stand still as a bat.

Can you believe it? The sun has come out,
And now it is full of light,
I am as happy as a king,
Everyone is cheerful and bright.

Lauren Bhaduri (9)
The Mount School

Untitled

In Dubai the sea is calm,
The sand is very hot.
You have to rush to the sea to cool your feet,
And it feels like walking on hot coals.

In the sea you can see small, transparent fish,
It feels like they invite you in,
Along with the fish and small crabs.

I jump on my bodyboard and drift around,
Looking down in the sea,
It is calm and it is peaceful,
I love Dubai.

Laurence Denton (10)
The Mount School

Patterns And Colour

Patterns on the sea - when the sun goes up and down
Patterns under the sea like the Great Barrier Reef in Australia,
There you can see the beautiful patterns and colour on the coral.

There are patterns and colour in an ancient tapestry,
They are on flowers and plants and trees.
They are in the galaxy with the sun and the Milky Way,
Then there's beautiful mist, twirling and swirling through the air,
And snowflakes twinkling and floating gently to the ground.
The wind, whistling and howling,
The beautiful patterns and colour of hot air balloons.

Oh how I love patterns and colour.

Fern Share (9)
The Mount School

My Pet Rabbit

I had a pet called Flopsey
We used to call him Mopsey
He was big and black
A funny fat chap
Who used to sit on Nan's lap

He used to scratch
And frighten the cat
We all loved him to sit on the mat
I will always love him even though he died
And on that day we cried and cried

Goodnight
God bless
And rest in peace
And may the Lord take your soul to keep.

Chloe Sharpe (8)
Upton Upon Severn CE Primary School

My Goldfishes

My fishes are gold like the sun,
And they like to have fun.
They swim all day,
Usually in May.
They have beautiful tails,
Not like whales.

My fishes' names are Candy and Bubble,
And they don't cause me any trouble.
They live in their tank,
Like their friend Frank.
They like to play with their toys,
And they don't make any noise.

They like their food
When they are in a good mood.
They like each other
As they haven't got a mother.
They look happy together,
And I will love them for ever.

Elena Ioannou (9)
Upton Upon Severn CE Primary School

Moving House!

The snail is moving house today!
Hip hip hooray
Tootling like a tortoise over rocks and stones
The African snail has no bones.
Leaving the track of silver behind for me to find
The track so slimy it sticks to my hand
Covers the African snail's land
I look for the home compost in tone
African snails have no phone!
I follow his track
And find his house still on his back.

Emily Gregory (8)
Upton Upon Severn CE Primary School

A Poem About Monkeys

Monkeys are brown
They hang upside down
They swing from tree to tree
They're as tall as your knee

They like to eat fruit
Their faces are so cute
They're playful and they like to have fun
And I bet they'd like to have a sticky bun

Some live in cages and some are free
I'd like to have one as a pet but Mum won't let me
They get into loads of trouble
When they get into trouble it's usually double

Monkeys come in all shapes and sizes
Most of them live in a zoo
I like monkeys, how about you?
I love monkeys but Mum says I act like one too.

Daniel Hopkins (9)
Upton Upon Severn CE Primary School

Seashells

I like throwing stones in the sea.
I like seeing waves crashing next to me
and sleeping under a tree.
I like feeling the breeze blowing over me
and I like going on a jet ski.
I like eating fish and chips
and licking my lips.
I like playing beach ball
even with people very tall.
I like diving in the deep blue sea
and I hate driving home.
When I get home I scream and cry
and I make pictures with the clouds in the sky.

Cody Stokes (9)
Upton Upon Severn CE Primary School

My Pet Sooty

He's a cat and his fur is black,
You wouldn't dare put him in your sack.
He's naughty and he likes to bite,
He never ever has a fight.
His name is Sooty, he's a rapping cat,
And he's even got a comfy mat.
He's fluffy and soft,
He would jump even if you coughed.

He has fish on a stick,
If you say ouch, he gives you a lick.
I've got scratches on my hand and scratches on my legs,
Be warned if he is on the toilet, run away, it smells.
He's very rough,
And he's always very tough.

He's a tiny little baby,
I'd let you stroke him maybe.
He's my puss and he's very silly,
He's lovely and beautiful.
But that's why I love him so.

Sarah Hopkins (9)
Upton Upon Severn CE Primary School

Cats And Dogs

Cats and dogs sleep all night
With their tails curling tight
In the morning they awake
And we make their breakfast

Cats and dogs like to play
Up and down they go all day
Miaowing and barking
Going inside for *tea!*

Billy Taylor (8)
Upton Upon Severn CE Primary School

My Pets

My hamster nibbles and nibbles,
My hamster tickles and tickles.
He never bites us,
And he adores a fuss.

My cat is not fat,
He does not have a hat.
He sits on the mat,
That's where he likes to have a pat.

My puppy is small and cute,
He barks but doesn't toot.
He loves to play
Every day.

My parrot has rather sharp claws,
But he doesn't have soft paws.
He copies what we say,
He eats birdseed not hay.

Jack Marklew (10)
Upton Upon Severn CE Primary School

My Brother Peter

My brother Peter has blond hair
He is always happy, without a care
My brother Peter has brown eyes
Likes wearing waistcoats and tying ties
My brother Peter loves veg and peaches
Does his work and likes his teachers
My brother Peter makes us laugh
He plays with his Action Man in his bath
My brother Peter loves boats and trains
And plays the PlayStation when it rains
I love Peter; he's my little brother
But I told Mum I don't want another.

Laura Morgan (8)
Upton Upon Severn CE Primary School

Cars

Cars, cars, cars,
Shiny and gold,
Bright and red,
Black tyres, silver wheels.

Cars, cars, cars,
Engines starting,
Sirens wailing,
Tooting horns.

Cars, cars, cars,
Cars on the motorway,
Cars in the town,
Cars, cars everywhere.

Cars, cars, cars,
Cars have names,
Ford, Porsche, Rover,
And my favourite, Subaru.

Nathan Parsons (10)
Upton Upon Severn CE Primary School

School Fashions

At school we all have fashions
It really drives me mad,
If you haven't any cool toys
You may get really sad.

There are hundreds of fashions
Cards, stickers and toys,
Girls soon get into it
And so do boys.

They have all gone out of fashion now,
I really don't know why,
I think it's better running around,
Tag, you're on, goodbye!

Jim Owen (9)
Upton Upon Severn CE Primary School

The Simpsons

My favourite show is The Simpsons,
I watch it every night,
I like the Hallowe'en specials,
They really give me a fright.

Marge and Homer as Mum and Dad,
Lisa's so good and Bart is so bad.
Maggie's the baby of this mad lot,
Grandpa's so old they left him to rot.

With Santa's Little Helper, and Snowball the cat,
Marge is so thin and Homer's so fat.
They make me laugh and make me smile,
Barney Gumble does belches that are so vile,.
They make me want to run a mile.

Montgomery Burns is the oldest man,
He takes and takes as much as he can,
He is a multimillionaire, but not a nice one,
Maggie shot him with Grandpa's gun.

There's Carl and Lenny and Smithers too,
Then there's the Flanders, too good to be true.
Ned loves the Bible, and his sons Rod and Tod,
Whenever there's a problem, he shouts, 'Ned to God.'

The police chief is Clancy, and he's a bit thick,
His son is called Ralph,
And Bart takes the mick.

So this is my poem, I think it's quite neat,
Read on, watch The Simpsons, you're in for a treat.

Emily Jade Gould (10)
Upton Upon Severn CE Primary School

Pets

In our house we have lots of different pets,
Big ones, small ones, whatever next?
We have four snugly cats and one white mouse,
All of these animals live in my house.

We have one black guinea pig called Ebony,
And six fat fish, who used to live in the sea.
I have a job, which is to feed our two birds,
Charlie and Ajax who can't speak any words.

If I'm not careful they may try to escape,
Right through the window and out of the gate.
So I have to be gentle, so this doesn't occur,
So I do it very quietly, so that I can hear the cat purr.

I love all my animals and they love me,
If you come to my house it's very plain to see.
But if my mum decides to buy any more,
I will have to leave my bed and sleep on the floor.

Elliott Dawe (9)
Upton Upon Severn CE Primary School

About My Dog

I have a dog, he's ever so silly
His favourite friend is a dog called Billy
He's got black and white hair
It whizzes through the windy air
He fights like a lion
His owner's name is Ryan
He likes bats
But he can't stand cats
He barks at the milkman
As loud as he can
He likes hot meat
But he dislikes wheat.

Ryan Westbrook (10)
Upton Upon Severn CE Primary School

When My Dog Went To Heaven

When I was seven my dog went to Heaven,
He used to swim in the River Severn,
I hope he still does in Heaven,
For evermore he will be four,
He will no longer be there scratching at the door.

When I was seven my dog went to Heaven,
His eyes were as bright as the stars at night,
His fur was as dark as the midnight sky,
He had big paws and rather sharp claws.

His name was Sunny, he cost me no money,
He looked rather funny,
He lived on honey
Now I am left with a bunny,
It is not funny because my dog has died.

Michelle Lockyear (10)
Upton Upon Severn CE Primary School

The Pony In The Storm

The wind did blow, the rain did pour,
The puddles sploshed on the soaken floor,
In the corner of the field in the middle of the night,
Stood a little black pony full of fright,
The thunder roared, the lightning flashed,
It hit a tree and down it crashed,
Then someone came to help him out,
He heard the gate, he heard a shout,
They lead him away out of the storm,
Into a stable lovely and warm,
A hot bran mash was waiting there,
To show the pony they really did care,
The straw was cosy he slept upon,
He stayed till morning when the storm was gone.

Jessica Short (10)
Upton Upon Severn CE Primary School

School Dinners

Monday's lunch we had bangers and mash,
The sausages were as tough as glass.
The peas were frozen, the mash was cold,
They even made this one boy bald.

Tuesday's lunch we had fish fingers and chips,
The chips were so hot they burnt my lips.
The fish was all rotten, it smelt like a sock,
And the chips were as hard as a rock.

Wednesday's lunch we had jacket and beans,
The beans were so old they were nearly green.
The jacket was lumpy, the stench was dire,
A girl found a sock in the deep fat fryer.

Thursday's lunch we had curry and rice,
The meat from the curry looked like dead mice.
And then I saw a sticky white ball,
Yuck, that was the rice, now I've seen it all.

Friday came I was no fool,
I had to get the day off school.
My stomach ached, my eyes were red,
I had to spend the day in bed.
I knew I needed to recover,
And had a long chat with my mother.
The medicine I needed most,
Was a lovely home cooked roast.

Jessica Hewlett (10)
Upton Upon Severn CE Primary School

My Football Poem

I like football quite a lot,
And I have a very powerful shot,
On my shirt I wear number 8,
And my manager thinks I'm great,
We do lots of training to keep us fit,
And play all our matches in a black and green kit,
I like taking a penalty kick,
And sometimes the ball feels like a brick.

If the ball is near to the opponent's goal,
You should hit it inside the 3 poles,
Corner kicks are taken from an angle,
But sometimes you end up in a tangle,
Our goalkeeper is the best,
He is that good he hardly needs a rest,
I want to play with lots of pride,
But at the moment I only play 7-aside.

At the end of the season we won the cup,
When we held it high, it went up and up,
After we won the cup there was a presentation,
And there was a massive celebration,
Our parents were so proud,
They were singing and shouting very loud,
When I got home I was really excited,
All my family were very delighted.

Josh Barnett (9)
Upton Upon Severn CE Primary School

Frosty The Dragon

Frosty the dragon,
Seems nice but actually she's vicious and ferocious.
She blows wintry frost,
Instead of scalding fire.

Her spikes are wavy but pointy,
Like the point of lightning,
Her claws are a bit curly and long,
Like witches' fingernails.

Teeth are like transparent, shiny, solid glass,
They sparkle in the night.
Her belly is shiny and glittery,
It is slippery and smooth like ice.

Frosty's eyes are like vicious droplets,
You can hear her breathing.

Tail - long and curly with semicircle spikes,
Starts off fat and gets thinner,
Wings are a dark aquamarine,
When they beat they make a loud noise.

She is an aquamarine colour on her head,
Neck, belly, legs, feet and tail.
Her spikes are the colour cobalt,
She is colossal.

Annabelle Dodd (8)
Upton Upon Severn CE Primary School

The Fire-Breathing Dragon

There once lived a dragon so shiny and red
Who went by the name of Fiery Fred.
If anyone walked past he'd scare them to death
By shooting out flames of very hot breath!

James Breeze-Stringfellow (8)
Upton Upon Severn CE Primary School

Birtie The Dragon

I know a jolly nice dragon,
His name is Birtie,
We love to play outside,
But he gets rather dirty.

Birtie is a friendly dragon,
He is really quite fine,
And when he watches telly,
He likes to drink some wine.

Birtie sleeps in the garage,
His tail sticks out the door,
When he gets his supper,
He always asks for more.

Birtie is my friend,
We have lots of fun,
My mum and dad frown,
Because they think he'll burn the house down.

Birtie is as green as the grass,
His wings are blue and shiny,
His tail is long and spiky,
And when he goes to bed,
He wraps it round his head.

James Treacy (8)
Upton Upon Severn CE Primary School

My Rabbit

I have a rabbit called BB
She always loves it when she sees me
She runs around in the run like a chimpanzee
She flees from bees as if she was on waterskis.

George Chapman (8)
Upton Upon Severn CE Primary School

Baby Dragon

If I'd go to
Pick a pet,
I would pick a *dragon*.
With rosy-ruby eyes that you can see
In the mist.
A cheeky smile on his face,
Sharp spikes on his back,
Transparent, marine wings
That can fly high.
Shiny sapphire scales
Which glisten in the moonlight.
Violet spiky claws
Which make
A crunchy sound
As he walks.
Slimy, slippery grey tail
That slithers in the starlight.
Red-hot spikes
On the end of the tail.
My dragon is a
Baby frost-breathing dragon.

Korinna Barnard (8)
Upton Upon Severn CE Primary School

Food

Food keeps you going all day
As they say,
Water keeps us alive
Basic food helps us to survive
But when it comes to eating for fun
Sausages and chips fills my tum,
A splash of ketchup and baked beans too,
That's probably enough for me and you.

Matthew Burt (8)
Upton Upon Severn CE Primary School

The Beautiful Game

Subs are waiting,
Ready to go,
Teams are ready,
For the whistle to blow,
Striker kicks, to the side,
He runs after, it's too wide,
Towards the goal, it's a bet,
He aims it hard, it's in the net.

Dirty faces,
Muddy knees,
Nasty tackles,
And referees,
The fans are clapping,
Full time's here,
And a second goal was very near,
The game is over,
The team feels proud,
Great entertainment,
For the crowd!

Tom Bottomley (9)
Upton Upon Severn CE Primary School

The Ice Dragon

There is a dragon with a ticklish tummy,
Who wants to grow up like his mummy.
Ultramarine are his droplet eyes,
And he likes to fly up in the skies.
He breathes out frost and ice,
And likes lots of cuddles as they're quite nice.
He flies on aqua-blue wings,
From up high in the sky he can see lots of things.

Hannah Barney (7)
Upton Upon Severn CE Primary School

It's That Time Of Year Again!

It all happened when I was ten,
Along came Christmas time again,
Presents, stockings, Christmas trees,
Mince pies, nuts, biscuits and cheese!

It all happened on Christmas Eve,
Down the chimney with a great big sneeze,
With a great big sack of presents on his back,
It's twelve months on, and Santa's back!

It's all now happening on Christmas Day,
Lots of children bright and gay.
Santa's returned to his wonderful wife,
Everyone rejoices the eternal life!

Kayleigh Dodd (10)
Upton Upon Severn CE Primary School

My Favourite Things

M y love for animals is so great,
Y et folks treat them bad and this I hate.

F urry creatures are cuddly and sweet,
A nd a panda bear I would like to meet.
V isiting China to see these creatures,
O f course I would like their black and white features.
U nder and over the ground I see,
R abbits, Mum's favourite it has to be.
I n our hutch we have Peter rabbit,
T ickling his ears is my best habit.
E ating his vegetables he likes best,

T aking straw to make his nest.
H appy I am to see goldfinches resting,
I nside our tree where they are nesting.
N ext to my bedroom in the morning I hear,
G oldfinches - red, gold and white,
S eeing their feathers, what a pretty sight.

Sophie Swann (8)
Upton Upon Severn CE Primary School

My Pet Cat Spennie

Spennie is my cat,
She is black and white and very fat,
She loves the taste of a big, juicy rat,
And leaves it on the doormat.

She scratches at the windowpane,
In order to get in again,
She turns around and walks down the lane,
She stares at next-door's big Great Dane.

She is very good at catching birds,
She rips them into tiny thirds,
Then she swallows it all in one,
Straight down into her chubby tum.

Spennie is the best,
Although she is a pest,
I can't imagine life without her,
Or the soft, sweet, cuddly feeling of her fur.

Spennie is my cat.

Sophie-Marie Price (8)
Upton Upon Severn CE Primary School

The Dragon

I once saw a dragon
As I sat in my wagon
Sharp, pointy scales
A very long tail
With raindrop-shaped eyes
With his long, wide wings he flies
He has very sharp teeth
And fire-breathing breath.

Rebecca Chamberlain (8)
Upton Upon Severn CE Primary School

Alien Invaders

The alien invaders came out of space
And landed in my back garden leaving not a trace.

The alien invaders came out of space
And landed on the rooftop
Searching for my baby brother Jake.

The alien invaders came out of space
Searching for a place to stay
Because their master kicked them out today.

The alien invaders came out of space
Looking for me in every place
Then eventually they found me
Behind the back garden fence.

The alien invaders took me to space
And strapped me up in a funny case
And zapped a laser over my face.

Before I knew it I was in my bed
Then I heard Mum, 'Lucy, breakfast.'
'Coming Mum,' I said.
I went downstairs for my breakfast
And from that day I saw red eyes
Glaring at me on the alien's face.

Kelsey Bannister (8)
Upton Upon Severn CE Primary School

Thank You

When I don't know what to do,
I lift my head and turn to you.
You wipe my eyes, you dry my tears,
You take away my darkest fears.
When I'm feeling down and blue,
You always know what to do.
Thank you for being there,
Loads of love and please take care.

Carianne Martin (10)
Upton Upon Severn CE Primary School

In The Wild

Animals running in the wild,
Fast running cheetahs chasing deer,
Graceful gazelles bounding free,
Big, spotty leopards waiting to pounce.

The biggest, proudest one of all,
Is hidden in the tall grass,
King of the jungle, the lion,
Is ready to chase and kill.

The sun beats down,
And dries up the grass,
The animals head to the waterhole,
And into great danger.

At nightfall the jungle is quiet,
Except for rustling in the bushes,
And the hooting of an owl,
All is still until the dawn of another day.

Chantelle Parsons (8)
Upton Upon Severn CE Primary School

The Arctic Dragon

One cold and frosty morn
Just about dawn
High on a freezing hill
A silvery-eyed dragon flew through the mist
His sharp claws shone
His prickly teeth glistened
And his powerful transparent wings slapped
High above the colossal mountains
He was no ordinary dragon
His breath blew ice and froze everything in sight
Then one cold night he curled up tight
And froze himself for all his life.

Ryan Hill (7)
Upton Upon Severn CE Primary School

My Teddy

I have a little teddy
Who at cycling is very steady
As this teddy learns to write
He might just learn how to stop a fight
When this teddy goes to school
He never ever breaks a rule
His favourite subject is colourful art
While at maths he's really smart
This little teddy's hobby, swimming it is
When he does butterfly he really does fizz
This little teddy's favourite food is pancakes
And he has a pet elephant, which makes the house shake
When my teddy goes to parties
He always comes back with a tube of Smarties
And on one ear he has not much hair
This teddy I'm telling you about, his name is Blue Bear.

Laurence James Astill (8)
Upton Upon Severn CE Primary School

My Uncles

My uncle Billy is very silly
He forgot his trousers and got chilly
My uncle Taft is just as daft
He tried to cross the road in a raft
My uncle Chad is raving mad
He acts like a little lad
My uncle Tolly is a total wally
When it's sunny he uses his brolly
My uncle Cutter is a complete nutter
He has custard instead of butter
My uncle Rooney is a first class loony
His favourite trick is doing a moony
My uncle O'Toole is a silly old fool
He believes leprechauns live in his pool
Of all these uncles my favourite one is my uncle Chad.

Bryn Jarvis (8)
Upton Upon Severn CE Primary School

Mountain Horse

I see a black horse running across the misty stream
I hear a swish of a mane
It's climbing up a white, snowy mountain
I try and catch it, but I fail
It races with the wind
Faster than the speed of light
Will I ever catch the mountain horse?
As it threads its way through streams and snow.

Martha Owen (8)
Upton Upon Severn CE Primary School

The Ice Dragon

The ice dragon is mellow and cool
And his wings are his flying tool
He flies across the icy pool,
His eyes glisten like a silver jewel.

He's smooth but sharp,
As gentle as the strumming of the angel's harp,
And his shadow is as dark as the darkest dark,
He's as tame and as soft as the swooping lark.

Hannah Broadbent (7)
Upton Upon Severn CE Primary School

My Dog

I once had a dog
His name was Bo
Wherever we went
He had to go
If ever we left him
He would bark all day
He would drive the neighbours mad
In every way.

Dale Willis (10)
Upton Upon Severn CE Primary School

The Four Seasons' Fairy

(Based on 'A Fairy and The Four Seasons')

Spring
The fairy sees the flowers grow
Like little soldiers in a row
At the bottom of my garden.

Summer
The fairy sits by the pond
This to see, I'm very fond
In my garden.

Autumn
The fairy curls up in a ball
Out of the wind by the wall
In my garden.

Winter
The fairy flies slow
In the snow
At the bottom of my garden.

Kara Beth Thomas (9)
Upton Upon Severn CE Primary School

Freeza

Once upon a time
There was a dragon called Freeza
All different shades of blue
Transparent sky-blue wings
Beautiful diamond eyes
Smooth, scaly skin on her body
Shimmering azure-blue on her body
And sea-blue
The end of her tail was sapphire.

Jessica Williams (8)
Upton Upon Severn CE Primary School

The Seaside

Along the sand
I look at my hand
I see a shell
That looks like a bell
I see the sea
And there's a stranded tree
I play in the waves
And look at the caves
I'm making a sandcastle
Like a castle
I'm on my way home
I'm all alone
Except for the sea and me!
Every time I visit the sea
It reminds me of that stranded tree.

Georgie McMullen (8)
Upton Upon Severn CE Primary School

Alton Towers

I am so excited I cannot sleep,
I close my eyes but I still peep.
It's time to go to Alton Towers,
I hope that Mum doesn't make me shower.

The roller coasters are really fast,
I am really speedy as I go past.
I hope I can go there for keeps,
Also hope the hot dogs are really cheap.

At the end of the day I am really sad,
My legs are aching really bad.
The day's been long but really good,
I would like to stay,
I really would!

Jacob Jones (8)
Upton Upon Severn CE Primary School

The Cricket Game

Warm, sunny and a lazy day
And the start of the big game
Spectators relaxing on pavilion seats
The coin's tossed
The field is ready.

In the middle of the game
Bowler bowls, wow a six!
The lift of people out of their seats
The batsman not scared
Bowler bowls again, four this time.

Nearly the end
The big score up
Last over, here goes
Bowler in, it's a catch
Spectators are lifted.

We win!

William St Leger-Chambers (8)
Upton Upon Severn CE Primary School

A Blazing Dragon

Hot dragon with blood-red eyes
Ornate tawny golden scales glistening on its back
Moody mountainous dragon stomping
Swaying, storming through the town
Colossal feet thud on the ground
With sapphire claws
Teeth like turrets that glow in the dark
Fiery, magenta, red-hot breath
Monstrous wings flapping up and down
Transparent, colourful like stained glass.

Hannah Simmons (7)
Upton Upon Severn CE Primary School

My Auntie And Uncle

My auntie is an ugly old hag,
She's so ugly on her head she wears a bag.
My auntie is as mean as an angry bear,
She's enough to give you a nightmare.

Her house is as dusty as a coal shed,
One day I went there and found a mouse in a bed.
Her car is as old as a dinosaur bone,
So old the wheels are made of stone.

My uncle on the other hand is nothing like his wife,
He loves to be outside with all the wildlife.
He's as jolly as a clown,
He's the happiest man in town.

He's as thin as a rake and extremely tall,
With a head the size of a basketball.
He works as a teacher at the local school,
The pupils like it when he acts the fool.

William Cullwick (9)
Upton Upon Severn CE Primary School

The Ice Dragon

The dragon breathes ice out of his mouth
His teeth cross over
His back is spiky
And his tail is curly
His wings wave in the air
His feet are spiky,
His skin is covered in scales
Out of his mouth comes ice to freeze the world.

Samantha Dewick (8)
Upton Upon Severn CE Primary School

Mother Nature

Trees and flowers bloom,
Pretty things can lead to a trance.
Mother Nature has lots of room;
To grow her beautiful plants,
Rhododendrons are beautiful too.

Plants like palm trees,
Roses and lilies too.
Mother Nature has her needs;
Flowers even grow by the sea blue,
Eucalyptus is very useful.

But sometimes things are used,
Mother Nature judges
To see if fruit is cruised;
On giant crate barges,
Over the English Channel.

Rhiannon Turner (9)
Upton Upon Severn CE Primary School

The Nice Ice Dragon

I once knew a dragon
His back was as lumpy as rocks
On his freezing crystalline feet
He wore several pairs of socks

His sparkling marine-blue body
Flashed brightly in the sun
Though he was mischievous and never grumpy
He always found life fun

His soft, warm smell was never creepy
In fact, it made me feel quite sleepy.

Yoseph Taha (8)
Upton Upon Severn CE Primary School

Untitled

Fiery dragon hovering in the night,
Swooping high, swooping low,
Flapping his wings very slow,
Up he goes, breathing smoke,
When he opens his mouth,
It's not a joke.

Raindrop eyes as he spies,
Tasty morsels to fry,
Long, thorny tail,
Whipping to and fro,
He's not having me for tea,
Come on, let's go!

Bethany Cooper (8)
Upton Upon Severn CE Primary School

Dragon Poem

My dragon is cold
She is violet and sky-blue
She is purple and sea-blue
She is also white as ice
She is helpful and nice
She has huge, leathery purple wings
She also likes to sing
She has wings that flap
She has scales that overlap
She has pretty pale blue eyes
Her tail is white and pointy
When she breathes her cave freezes over.

Amy Miles (7)
Upton Upon Severn CE Primary School

Spooky Boot

I saw a monster in the woods
As I was cycling by,
His footsteps smouldered in the leaves,
His breath made the brushes die.
And when he raised his hairy arm,
It blotted out the sun,
He snatched a pigeon from the sky
And swallowed it in one.
His mouth was like a dripping cave,
His eyes were like pools of lead,
And when he growled I rode back home,
And rushed upstairs to bed.
But that was yesterday and though
It gave me quite a fright,
I'm older now and braver,
So I'm going back tonight.
I'll tie him up when he's asleep
And take him to the zoo,
The trouble is he's rather big,
Will you come too?

Matthew Bromwich (10)
Upton Upon Severn CE Primary School

Dean The Fire Dragon

A long time ago there was a dragon
Who was huge, selfish, angry and mean
Who had sharp and spiky teeth and whose name was Dean
He smashed his way about with a fearless scowl
With a smell that followed him which was most foul
If he caught anything he liked, he'd either roast or boil it with
                                            his flaming breath
Then he would roar at you loudly until you went deaf
So stay out of his way and walk about quietly
And remember this when you go to bed nightly.

George Dawe (7)
Upton Upon Severn CE Primary School

My Icy Dragon

Some dragons can be scary
Big and fiery
But my dragon is kind
And his friendship is hard to find.

He stands so tall
With strength and pride
His powerful wings
On either side.

His transparent wings are edged in pale blue
His body is sapphire and white
His scales are multicoloured
Aqua, indigo and marine too.

He will be my friend
From morning till night
Keeping me safe
With all his might.

Oliver Storr (8)
Upton Upon Severn CE Primary School

Mysterious Dragon

As I stood and stared,
The ice dragon started
To move his cobalt eyes,
Which made me feel like ice,
It felt so cold,
It made me feel so old.

I know I shouldn't be in this place,
And as the ice dragon breathes,
I feel like an iced frozen plate,
As I start to freeze.

Alfie Owen (7)
Upton Upon Severn CE Primary School

Sweets

Sweets, we're just treats
But you can't sing songs
Brown, black and long
Better than pie *or* I
So don't cry
Just try
Until it's night
Because you *might* get a terrible fright
It's better than beer
So see here
O dear
It all goes in my multicoloured head
All different colours - blue, black, grey or red
But now it's time for bed
So clean your teeth or you won't get any more
Sweet treats!

Alister Stevens (9)
Upton Upon Severn CE Primary School

Dragon Poem

In a dark forest where nobody goes,
You can hear a crashing sound that nobody knows.
Ginormous footprints are left behind,
To a fearless dragon which is unkind.
He is yellow, he is green,
You might think that he is unclean.
A spiky back and fierce teeth,
Watch out, you may get some grief.
His body smells of rotten eggs,
And he blows hot flames at your legs.
If you see this evil dragon,
Run away or catch a wagon.

Tim Lewis (7)
Upton Upon Severn CE Primary School

Dragon

When I was curled up in my bed,
I saw a fire-breathing dragon,
Who was blood-red.
He was very, very scary,
And I was very wary.
His bad tempered eyes,
So rosy-red,
His wings are even bigger than my bed.
His mighty powerful tail,
Knocked over my glass whale,
Then I woke up screaming,
And Mum said, 'You're only dreaming.'

Bethan Howells (8)
Upton Upon Severn CE Primary School

My Dragon

My dragon is hot
He breathes flames that are boiling hot
He has pointy toes
He has a big green nose
His body is pale orange
His tail is creamy-white
He has big wings to help with flight
His teeth are shiny white
They are pointy like mountains
His wings are huge and yellow
His favourite food is marshmallow.

Anthony Miles (7)
Upton Upon Severn CE Primary School

If I Was A Bird

If I was a bird I would fly from my troubles
Leave all my woes behind
I would fly to Africa, Spain or Greece
Until a better land I would find.

I would swoop down on my prey
Without a single sound
Gather up bundles of twigs
And make a nest cosy and round.

I would sit on the nest
King of the air
I would lay some eggs
Who were to be my heirs!

If I was a bird.

Harry Maher (9)
Winterfold House School

My Cat

My cat is small and fluffy
She will snuggle anywhere
Or sleep in an armchair
Dreaming of milk and mice
Her paws twitching here and there
Whiskers moving to and fro
Eyelids flickering.

When my cat wakes up
She stretches and washes herself
Makes gentle movements
Scampers to her milk bowl
Then off she goes to find the mice
From the wonderful dreams she had.

Jo Dearden (10)
Winterfold House School

A Beautiful Tiger

A tiger is truly beautiful
With its stripy coat
If you see one swaying its tail
It's got to be a female
If you see one biting its prey
You really should run away

Tigers may look very cute
But deep down inside they're very fierce
They look beautiful with their black stripes
And wonderful orange fur
A tail like a swan's neck
And dazzling whiskers like shiny hair

A tiger could be prowling in the jungle
Or drinking from a wonderful lake
It could be mating and raising its cubs
Or licking its fur to make it shine
It could be chasing its prey
Oops! There it goes! Better try another day.

Annie Jenkinson (9)
Winterfold House School

Dragons Roaring

Dragons roaring
Gliding and slithering
Lighting the sky with fireballs like lightning
Scales of fire glistening in darkness

Gorgan hissing
Biting and growling
Turning her enemies into mindless stone
Snapping and snarling
Until they are dead.

Charlie Muir (9)
Winterfold House School

Mythical Beasts

The Cyclops is a mythical beast,
They are known to be good shepherds,
They have one big eye,
That looks a bit suspicious.

Medusa is a snake-like beast,
With each of her hairs a snake,
Just take one glance,
And you're in a frozen stance,
But I'm glad she's only fake.

Pegasus the white flying horse,
He sparkles in the darkness of night,
He looks beautiful in the wonder of its flight,
Pegasus the white flying horse.

Charlie Green (10)
Winterfold House School

The Cyclops

Dreams of a land of mythical beasts
A strange place, full of monstrous creatures
Out of the mist came a terrifying monster
One-eyed Cyclops
From his lair, a dark, creepy cave
The ugliest of creatures emerged
To eat his favourite food
Raw human beings
The Cyclopes' huge teeth
Snap the humans in half
Then he grinds their bones into tiny bits
Sometimes the Cyclops
Will swallow you whole
To die in his stomach
If you dare walk on his land
You may never return.

Harry Nuttall (10)
Winterfold House School

Daedalus And Son

Daedalus and son were in the tower
To go home was their dearest dream
The king said no
But Daedalus said, 'We must go,'
And what a good plan it did seem.

To make wings of wax to fly away
To their homeland and freedom once more
But Daedalus's son ignored his father's advice
And straight to the sun he did soar.

His wings got hotter and melted away
And into the sea he did fall
Like a stone and drowned
He should have done as he was told
And ended safe and sound.

Ginny Brewer (9)
Winterfold House School

The Sky

The sky is a great blue portal, opening the way to space and beyond,
Littered with birds and clouds,
Like a great illusion,
A mystery,
A lake strewn with white stones,
The eighth wonder of the world.

The sky is like a great breath of air,
Silent, yet still huge,
A giver of life,
The lungs of the Earth,
The world would die without it.

Tim Atkinson (10)
Winterfold House School

Flight

A passenger plane soars, slicing through the air
Travelling to new places
Through the clouds you can see
A tiny speck in the blue
Exciting destinations lie ahead

The glider, creepily floats in the air
Staying silent, just like an eagle
Slowly, swirling around
Like a spider crawling up its web
Circling its prey

The war plane's speed rises
Destruction in its wake
Devastation is what people expect
For like strong gales and powerful storms
It cannot be stopped, it will not be stopped
A terrible menace!

Julien Petitjean (10)
Winterfold House School

The Sky

The sky has many moods
And changing colours
Light blue for happiness
Sun shining lighting up the sky
White for gentleness
Snowflakes falling softly making no sound
Grey when it is sad
Rain falling like tears
Dark blue when it is sleepy
No light except for the moon's beam
Black when it is angry
Thunder crashing with mighty force
The sky has many moods.

Kate Robbins (9)
Winterfold House School

Flight

Soaring above the Earth,
Breaking through fluffy white clouds,
Piercing a hole in the sky,
Leaving a trail of white,
Flying at supersonic speeds,
Speeding over the ocean,
Zooming round the world,
Just some of the joys of flying today!

But it wasn't always like this,
The first flight was short,
At a low altitude with spluttering engines,
But still it must have been great,
To be the first to experience,
The freedom of the air,
Air rushing over the wings,
A bird's eye view of the land.

Alex Willson (10)
Winterfold House School

Space

Ploughing through everlasting space,
Galaxies on their continuous course,
Through the vastness of the universe,
Eternal space,
Unlimited universes,
Empty space,
Light of infinite stars,
Illuminating darkness,
Reflecting off planets,
Revealing the furthermost reaches of the universe,
Black holes destroying it forever,
Casting darkness back,
Each galaxy emitting its light to others,
Trying to illuminate the blackness!

Nicholas Radcliffe (10)
Winterfold House School

The Sky

The sky is blue, orange and black,
Sometimes purple, pink or grey.
When the sky is happy,
The sun comes out.
But when sad, it rains,
It's dull and grey.
When angry, it roars with thunder,
Flashes with lightning,
And black clouds appear.
When the sky is calm,
Clouds drift by,
All fluffy and white.
When laughing,
Snow falls like a butterfly.

The sky has beautiful sunsets,
With red, orange and yellow,
With a smudge of pink.
When the sun shines through the clouds,
A ray of light is set free.

The sky has different colours,
Moods and pictures.

Belle Watson (10)
Winterfold House School

Concorde

C ourageously crashing through the air
O nly to be oblivious about the world around it
N othing stands in its way but fluffy white clouds
C arrying people to glorious countries
O verlooking mountain ranges or tropical rainforests
R ivers on the ground flash by
D iving into land at the end of the journey
E ventually landing, the adventure is over.

Alex Attwood (10)
Winterfold House School

Mission Mars

In the spaceship 'Three Stars'
We travelled towards Mars.
Through the space we zoomed
And the rocket engines boomed.

We looked out at the black sky
As onwards we did fly.
Through meteor showers and rock
Which bashed the ship and made the doors knock.

Then on the left we spotted
A galaxy where stars were dotted.
Spiralling towards us was a dark mass
Which looked like poisonous gas.

The captain pushed the main switch
But suddenly there was a glitch.
The motors stopped humming
And the black hole kept coming.

Panicking we felt ourselves slide
Like being pulled by a big tide.
We saw the winking stars disappear
And in our last moment we shed a tear.

Duncan Keir (10)
Winterfold House School

Fireworks

The flaming fireworks are shooting up in the sky
They are squirting out pretty colours ever so high
The colours are twinkling like swirling flowers
There's so many they could fill up tumbling towers
It sounds like a booming crash
It feels like an extremely hot rash!
It looks like a fizzing rose against the black night
Guy Fawkes on the bonfire - what a dazzling sight.

Olivia Foulds (9)
Winterfold House School

Dipping And Diving

Flying, an amazing experience,
Dipping and diving,
Spinning and soaring,
Flight is a wonderful feeling,
Faster than sound,
Leaving a trail of fluffy white foam,
Which the whole world can see.

Butterflies in your stomach,
As you lift off, climbing into the clouds,
Once you are up there,
Among the birds,
Spectacular views amaze you,
And you are set free,
By the magical feeling.

Max Hunter (10)
Winterfold House School

Fish Poem

No arms but a fin
And scales for skin
His home is a bowl
Is he a lonely soul?

Swimming in the open sea
As fast as a fish can be
Watch out for the fisherman's net
Or doom will surely be met.

Served up on a dish
Is a beautiful fish
Surrounded by chips and peas
A long way from the ocean seas.

Jonathan Newbould (7)
Winterfold House School

The Alien

The sky shrouded in mist,
Wind howling furiously.
Lightning bulleted around the sky,
Rain cascading.

A strange humming sound,
Filled the air.
An unusual buzzing.
A craft was landing,
Oval and silver,
Gleaming and glistening.
Emerging from the spaceship,
Drifted a creature.

Bright green with purple spots,
Devilish red eyes,
No ears
But teeth like daggers
And a body full of hair!

The invasion had begun
'We have come to take over your planet!'

Daniel El-Dalil (11)
Winterfold House School

A Rainbow Poem

Rainbows are really pretty
And they are very colourful too
They make people very happy
They create a beautiful hue.

Rainbows show up in rain and sun
And children are always told
Come quickly when they show
To find their pot of gold.

Georgia Warner Tomlinson (8)
Winterfold House School

Up In Space

Looking through the window,
Up in space
I see stars drifting further away,
I see planets unknown to man.
The vast universe surrounds me.

There is no sound,
Other than our rocket.
Back behind us we see Earth.
It is peaceful up in space.

A spaceship hovers above us,
On its way to another galaxy.
The spaceship was spectacular,
Way before our time.
With a blast,
It disappeared from sight.

In the distance,
I can see
A thing destroying everything.

Our time was up,
Our journey done.
We hastened back,
From whence we came.

Rupert Buchanan (10)
Winterfold House School

A Rainbow Poem

R ain and sun shines through the light
A mazed with colours so bright
I ndigo the brightest colour glowing
N ever could I find where it is going
B elow the rainbow
O ver the clouds
W here the pot of gold is to be found.

Grace Stringer (8)
Winterfold House School

When I Grow Up

When I grow up I'll be an astronaut,
and be the first to land on Mars,
I'll own an alien called Flaut,
And feed him chocolate bars!

When I grow up I'll be a pilot,
And be abducted into space,
I'll catch an alien called Kilot,
And show him to the human race!

When I grow up I'll be an explorer,
And explore the seven seas,
I'll find a horrible monster,
And conquer him with ease!

When I grow up I'll be an astronomer,
And discover a new solar system,
I'll call it 'System Alistair',
And be admired for my wisdom!

When I grow up I'll be an inventor,
And be pulled into a new galaxy,
I'll examine that galaxy's meteors,
And be back in time for tea!

Harriet Alford (10)
Winterfold House School

The Frightful Night

Bats hanging, flying, black shapes.
Foxes sneaking, creeping, howling.
Moon beaming, shining, silver.
Stars glitter silently.
Shadows moving dark and creepy,
Dark shapes loom and threaten.
Things mysterious, frightening and hanging.
Clouds huge and making shadows.
That is what my night looks like!

Joshua Passmore (9)
Winterfold House School

Aliens - Two Points Of View

Aliens!
What frightening things!
Giant spiders,
With bulging eyes
And fangs for teeth,
Dripping slime as they hunt for human prey,
Crawling along menacingly
Destroying everything in their way
Only interested in human flesh.
They want to take us over!

Aliens!
What friendly little things!
ETs
With long-lashed eyes
And wide-open mouths
Surprised at the wonders of this human Earth.
Scuttling around excitedly,
They befriend everyone,
Coming in peace
Interested in learning about this Earth
Intent on exploration.

Fiona McHugh (11)
Winterfold House School

A Rainbow Poem

R ainbows shine high up in the sky
A mazed, it's just like you want to be there
I t's just so shiny and colourful
N earer you reach, you might touch it
B lue the colour of the great big sky
O ver and over it towers above the houses
W e light up when we see a rainbow.

Danny Kalloghlian (8)
Winterfold House School

Space

Way up in the dark sky,
Shooting through the dark.
Are we going to the moon
Or are we on our way to Mars?
I have no way to know
I am an astronaut soaring on my way
The aim is to get there
But will it be today?

The mission is space,
The dark unknown.
Am I in Apollo?
Or just on my own?
I am weightless,
I feel no sense of ground,
I am like a gymnast, whirring around.

I hear my name,
By the sound of a familiar voice,
'Where am I?
Where am I?' I ask
I open my eyes to look into a familiar face,
Home!

Tom Westley (10)
Winterfold House School

Snow

The snow is like white paint
The snow is crystal clear
It's as cold as the North Pole
It's as white as sugar.

The snow falls from the sky in white balls
It can freeze things up
The snow suddenly melts away.

James Thornton (11)
Winterfold House School

Friends

Hey there's my pony outside
And she's getting ready for me to ride
She's walking round and round the gate
She's looking like she thinks I'm late
I check the time and my pony's right
And to me that isn't a very good sight
I call my mum but she's still asleep
So I go to her room and take a peep.

The buzzer goes, hey Grace is here
My mum wakes up well that's clear
Why is she here? My mum asks me
I told her to come at half-past three.

It's only half-past twelve now
Why's she so early? I wonder how
I get dressed fast and run outside
To see George tacked up and ready to ride
I go to Crunchie and get her in
But she looks muddy, where has she been?
I think she has got out again
Like yesterday at half-past ten
Enough about that let's get ready to ride
I'm telling you Grace this pony will glide.

So off we go into the wood
Why don't we go in the field?
I think we should
I don't think we should, we're halfway through
But George is tired, well that's true
Let's have a canter, come on let's go
But George is tired and his energy's low
You need to get him going
For tomorrow he is showing
Wee hee let's go
I think he's good enough for a show
We'd better get back it is time for lunch
Come on then George, come on Crunch.

Yum-yum this is nice
What is it Mum? Is it rice?
Oh look at her out there eating her lunch
Look at my pony, look at Crunch
Where is George? I asked Grace
He's over there, he likes his own space
'Neigh,' says Crunch, 'Neigh,' says George
Oh look at him, look at Georgie Porge.

Jessica Dunn (8)
Winterfold House School

Space

Stars soaring past me,
The spaceship humming
As it hovers over Earth.

Inside it is metallic
Covered in switches and levers
And a weird computer settled in the corner.

The spaceship is as wide as a football pitch
And as high as buildings.
The spaceship's the colour of silver.

Stars shimmer past me,
As I stare out of the window
At the vastness we call space.

The aliens are approaching me
And talking in a strange language
I think they're talking about me.

I want to go home but I'm stuck here
Not allowed to go home
Stuck in this crazy world.

Elizabeth Hawkley (11)
Winterfold House School

The Delightful Dolphin

I think my favourite holiday would be
beside the sea
where I could swim with dolphins
and they could swim with me.

Dolphins are so beautiful
they're fun and cheeky too
I love to hear the song they sing
from deep within the ocean blue.

I think it's very funny
when they choose not to behave
and I love to watch them jumping
in and out of all those waves.

It's lovely to see the dolphins jump
it's such a pretty sight
I love dolphins so much
that they would never bite.

Abbie-May Griffiths (8)
Winterfold House School

A Spaceship

Last night I saw a UFO
In the shape of a test tube
It made a humming noise
It landed with a quiet bump
Doors opened with a shower of smoke
Levers, switches, cogs and control panel were revealed

Weird creatures said they were from Mars
Their friends would be here soon
They told me that their ship had lights
They said they've got a planet recognition system
They also said their ship was metallic.

Thomas Blakeway (10)
Winterfold House School

Bonfire Night

Late at night
All around is bright
Yellows, reds, blues and whites
Fireworks in the sky high as kites
Children stand and stare
Wrapped in coats and gloves
Brave the cold night air
Everyone watching Guy Fawkes burn
The bonfire lies in ashes
But next year it will return.

Charles Newbould (9)
Winterfold House School

Limerick

There was a young Viking from Oslo
Who was just that little bit slow
When out on his boat
All he could do was float
Hence was only able to go with the flow.

Annabelle Ward (9)
Winterfold House School

Fireworks

Exciting colours flying
At night making such a pretty sight
See sparklers making names
Having fun and playing games

Rockets flying from ground to sky
Bangs making babies cry
Catherine wheels spin round and round
Making a funny whistling sound.

Oliver Dunn (9)
Winterfold House School

My Mission

We landed.
Sinking our moon boots into the surface.
The engine was still purring.
Earth's waters glistening.
A huge ship hurtled towards me.
Out of the blue from behind the Earth more came.
Joining their leader.
In a circle they leered down at me and the ship.

A beam stared at me.
There was one thing to do.
Run.
To the nearby ship.
I made it by a whisker.
Now I must get back to Earth.
There were UFOs on my back.
The chase was on.

I started the engine, stalled.
I raced to an individual capsule, jammed.
What could I do.
I anticipated their arrival behind a barrel of food, nothing.
While I waited I had no idea the ship was being surrounded.
All I could think was *death*,
All I could feel was *death*,
All I could hear was a poisoning *death*.

I heard a gentle pitter-patter coming down the corridor.
I crept back ready to bolt when . . .
I was seized by something,
Now more and more and more.
My mission to find life on the moon.
Has been marred by things,
I never knew could exist.

Christian Lowe (11)
Winterfold House School

The Friggydight

Have you seen a friggydight?
The meanest monsters that put up a fight,
Standing at seven feet tall,
A bit like an ant, doesn't crawl
They're covered in hair like a dog
But can jump as high as a giant frog.

These beasts will only eat,
Just vegetables and no meat
They're really quite shy,
But with their manners I wonder why
With thick legs and arms and a dog-like tail
The things they eat make me pale.

And so that is the friggydight
That mysterious character that wonders the night
He's the gruesome guy that scares us all
The strong creature that will never fall
For he is hiding all day
And who knows, they could be here to stay!

Harry Radford (11)
Winterfold House School

Snow

The snow was like mushy clouds,
Thick, fluffy and glistening,
Covering the driveway,
Snow powder on the rooftops,
Flaky cotton wool shapes,
On the flowers and trees.
The path rippled by footprints,
Hills topped with whippy ice cream
Touching the clouds.

Jak Warren (11)
Winterfold House School

The Red-Eyed Monster

The car whizzed down the street
Accelerating at maximum speed
But it was not faster than the beast.

Its eyes were bright red
Its body a dark black
Where had this fiend come from?
Did anyone know?

It landed with force
The car went off course
It went straight into a tree
And started to burn horrifically

The beast leapt into the air
And spread its magnificent wings
Casting shadows below

It glided gracefully
And swooped down
Plucking the car from the road
It let out an ear-piercing screech
And shot off
Through the forest
Its razor-sharp claws
Scraping the treetops.

Joseph Humfress (10)
Winterfold House School

Snow

Snowflakes falling softly
Covering the ground lightly
Shining oh so brightly
In the sunlight
Glistening brightly
All day and night.

Braden Jeavons (11)
Winterfold House School

A Trip To Planet Earth
(As an alien's point of view)

Floating weightlessly through the air,
Looking at outer space, in a bewitched stare.
Twinkling planets and stars zoomed by,
In the darkness of the sky.

Over the control panels, I did see,
A strange planet of what seemed to be.
Patches of blue, patches of green,
Could it be the planet of strange aliens we've seen?

Suddenly in a crashing smash of light,
Something shook the ship with a fright.
Sucked down to the floor, we were,
Not to hear the sound of the engine purr.

Glad I was, we went no more near,
As already, I started to shake with fear.
Never again I will venture into that part of space,
It was a frightening experience going to that place.

George Mitchell (10)
Winterfold House School

Gentle Blackness

Night is just a peaceful thing,
only silver light does the moon bring.
Owls hoot softly from black trees,
rivers swirl gently brought by subtle seas.
Although there's nothing to harm you out there,
you can get a horrid scare.
But it's barely anything, just your cat,
or a fluttering dark black bat.
Finally shimmering dawn breaks through,
showing everything coloured and new.

Sophie Grenfell (8)
Winterfold House School

Inside A Spaceship

Inside a spaceship it's all different.
Nothing's outside, just stars and the everlasting universe.
Bare planets, no life.
Things all in one special place,
The universe.

Endless corridors,
Full with vapour and smoke.
Metallic walls with no end.
Cogs, switches, levers,
All on the side of a corridor.
All these things with nobody using them,
In a long, neglected corridor.

All you can hear is the sound of throbbing engines,
But with faint background of a whirring, humming sound.
Windows showing the stars, planets, black holes, comets,
All beautiful things,
That are in our home,
The universe.

Sam Hornsey (10)
Winterfold House School

Night

N ow it is night, dark shadows out.
I shiver in the howling wind.
G roans in the darkness.
H owling winds blow the trees . . .
T he branches like hands.

S hifting shadows
H owling winds move the trees like a monster waiting to pounce.
A ll is black, things creep across the sky
P eople sleep in their beds, unaware of the shadows.
E ach one in their shadow.
S hivering in their own dreams.

Alistair Evans (8)
Winterfold House School

Delicate Snow

It was silent in the park
And at midnight all was dark
I looked up and saw clouds puffy white
Snow's on the way and I was right.

Tiny flakes had changed the weather
Falling to the ground like a velvet feather
In the whiteness was a crystal flake
When it came down, it didn't want to break.

Sparkling jewels soon covered the ground
But only my footprints could be found
Powdery snow sprinkling as far as I can see
Even on the birds hiding in the tree.

When the snow stopped it was like a white sheet
Enough to build a snowman without any feet
My face tingling as the air was cold
I love delicate snow as much as gold.

Harriet Finney (10)
Winterfold House School

Snow

The brightness of the moon
Cuts through the darkness of the night
Into the soft slippery snow
Like dancers through the light

As cold as the Ice Age
That penetrates the ground
Like the flow of lava
Without the slightest sound

But underneath the snow
Like a warm pillow
That cushions all the life
Until the spring when it will glow.

Michael Boszko (10)
Winterfold House School

A Rainbow Poem

R ain or sun it shines its light
A mazed and dazzled by this wonderful sight
I ndigo, violet, bright colours glowing
N ever do we know where it is going
B elow this beautiful shining rainbow
O ver the hills it disappears in full flow
W here is the pot of gold? Let it show.

Ellie Pagan (8)
Winterfold House School

A Rainbow Poem

R ainbows in the sky
A nd we never see their end
I ndigo and violet
N ow it fades though it glows
B eauitiful stripes of amazing light
O ver the hill it stretches far, far away
W hen it's gone we are sad even though it will come again.

Millie Kiosses (9)
Winterfold House School

Fireworks

F izzling friendly fireworks
I gnited and iridescent.
R ed-hot rockets rising
E lectric effects in the sky
W histling, waiting for sound
O range, yellow, gold and silver
R ainbows raining down
K ids holding hands to ears
S creaming, splattering, smashing, *fireworks!*

James Douglas-Osborn (9)
Winterfold House School

Blizzard

The blizzard turning, twisting, never stopping
Laughing, dancing, clouds falling
Crispy, moody, grabbing wind, robbing
Stealing happiness from the sun

Animals hiding from the killing hand
Trees falling, people calling
Snow playing, ponds freezing, fish dying
People slipping on the ice

Gritters failing, getting stuck in the snow
The sun fading into the distance
Blizzards never-ending, ruling the world
People giving up hope

Finally the snowing stops, winds dying
The war is over
The sun takes control again
It's over until next time.

George Painter (10)
Winterfold House School

The Sky

The sky is home to the weather
And is blue in colour.
The plane cuts it in half,
As if it were a knife through butter.

The plane is streamlined in shape
And has a nose quite pointy,
Passing colourful birds
On the way to another country.

The birds have arrived in Africa,
The hottest place on Earth.
Greeted by foreign people,
The people who don't like to surf.

Lewis Martins (9)
Winterfold House School

Snow

It is getting dark
The clouds begin to gather.
Everything is as white as paint
It is covering the heather.

It's as cold as ice
But still looks nice.
Let's have a snowball fight
And dance all night.

Emily Heron (11)
Winterfold House School

A Snowy Experience

I woke up in the morning and I saw the snow
It filled me with excitement and made me glow.

I ran outside to explore this bright, cold, new world
I turned around to feel a snowball being hurled.

It hit me in the face and slid down my T-shirt
I thought to myself, *those boys will eat dirt.*

So much to my shocked surprise no boys could I see
It was the snow that was falling off the oak tree.

Kristian Marcus (10)
Winterfold House School

A Rainbow Poem

R ain is definitely in the air
A mazing colours appear
I 'd like to meet the start or end
N earer no; it's still around the bend
B ecause it is such a beautiful sight
O ver our heads the bridge takes flight
W here it lands, I'll search with all my might.

Ben Salsby (9)
Winterfold House School

Sparklers

S parkling in front of my eyes
P erishing in the dark
A nd the real smoky smell
R eally good fun
K indle the flame
L ight fading away
E xciting
R unning around making shapes
S ee the red glow.

Emma Westley (8)
Winterfold House School

Archie

There was a dog called Archie
And a handsome young Labrador was he.
One day he ran off
And some sausages he did scoff,
Before returning to his loving family.

Lydia Brindley (9)
Winterfold House School

A Rainbow Poem

R aindrops are such gorgeous things
A mazing colours creating a bridge
I n and out of the rain it goes
N othing compares to its beauty
B right lights in the dark sky
O n the horizon its colours dazzle
W hen the rainbow comes there is magic again.

Alexander Buckley (8)
Winterfold House School

My Poem About Snow

Snow is falling cold and white.
The snow is coming, filling me with fright.

His snowy fingers grab my feet
And cause my heart to miss a beat.

How this cold does make me chill
The monster's grasp does make me ill.

As it crawls back into the night
It gives me one last fright.

Jack Brehaut (11)
Winterfold House School

The Snow Poem

The snow stinging like a swarm of bees
And clutching at my face and my feet
And the snow, cold, fast and icy
Dangerous and slippery, wet
And glistens in the sun as it melts.

Bart Brierley (10)
Winterfold House School

The Curse Of The Snow

Those long glacial fingers ripping at my flesh,
Consuming my heat,
With a cold and icy hex.

That white death coating the ground,
Starving all the natural world,
Animals and plant life,
Big and small.

Freezing moisture with its icy anger,
In retribution for the evil in the world,
Laying its blanket to suffocate sin.

Sam Rudge (11)
Winterfold House School

Space

Space is a wonderful thing
Its black holes
So dark like midnight
Its shooting stars
So bright like the sun
So fast
And all its planets
So vast
And only one
Is inhabitable
Earth.

All the galaxies
So big
And so many of them
Each planet
So vast
And empty
The Milky Way
Our galaxy
Our home
Its vastness
So great
Is our galaxy
It holds us
In its centre
Along with the solar system
And some day
We will explore all of this.

It's an enormous place out there
You know, and it will be explored.

Andrew Dowty (10)
Winterfold House School

Snow

The snow's cold crystals bit into my hand
I crunched it into a ball
And threw it at my snowman
Who was so small
Smallest of all
Was mine.

Hooray!
The flakes started to fall
Soon my ball was covered in it all.

Crunch! I crushed the snow beneath my feet
Like a cotton blanket
It lay over the garden
Every step was exciting
It was such a rare experience.

Edward Cartwright (10)
Winterfold House School

Snow

I woke up one frosty morning to see snow falling
The whole garden was covered in white, fresh snow
I rushed to get dressed in warm woolly clothes
In black wellington boots to protect my toes

I went into the garden
My footsteps following me
I am going to build a snowman
As big as can be

I worked very quickly and soon it was complete
I ran back into my house to collect a scarf and hat
My Mr Snowman will look very smart in that!

Louis Pagan (10)
Winterfold House School

Snow

The playground was
A blanket of thick
Suffocating snow.
Very much like a sea of foam,
As crunchy as a crunchy sweet.

It makes the countryside wild.
All of a sudden
The wind freezes.
What's going on?
The snow curls up like a snake.
Snowballs abound wherever you walk.
Everywhere we go we see footprints.
Hang on the ponds are frozen;
Let's go skating.

Fern Brewer (11)
Winterfold House School

The Snow

The white velvet sheet,
Grabbing at your feet,
You can't resist to go,
Out into the snow.

The cold fluffy wool,
A giant charging bull,
It gets in the way,
All through the day.

The giant snowstorm,
It's definitely not warm,
It's travelling through the land,
And wrecking things hand in hand.

Gregg Wookey (10)
Winterfold House School

The Snowman

I was walking one day,
In the crisp, floury, white snow,
When I saw a snowman.
He was big and round,
I felt him, he was like ice cream.
When the sun shone against his body,
It was like crystal.

His nose was sharp as a knife,
His eyes were as round as a plate,
I thought in my head,
If only he was real,
I would stick to him, like glue.

Natalie Kalloghlian (11)
Winterfold House School

Night

In the shadowy night
I sometimes get a fright
When spiders are creeping
And we are all sleeping
Clouds of grey scuttle by
While owls screech and fly
All the dead people outside in their graves
Come out in ghostly waves
I am really scared I can't get to sleep
But instead I weep
But when the sun comes up and the moon comes down
I am not scared anymore because it's morning in the town.

Georgia Meredith (9)
Winterfold House School

Dear Diary

Today at school
It went really bad
I couldn't do anything
I was really sad.

I fell off my chair
I whacked my head
I was really embarrassed
I turned bright red.

I splattered the paint
All over the floor
I really couldn't take it
Any more.

My pencils broke
As I fell in the bin
My heart was pumping
As hard as a tin.

In the playground
I fell in the mud
I hurt my knee
As I landed with a thud.

Everyone laughed
They were having fun
But I was not
I was the only one.

I felt really small
As I walked home from school
And now I'm in bed
I can't be a fool!

Kelly Wilkinson (11)
Witton Middle School

The Sea Is A Grizzly Bear

The sea is a grizzly bear, lumbering up the beach,
Poking his sharp claws into the sand,
Trying to stay on the land,
But getting swept out of his reach.

On stormy days, in bounds the bear,
His coat silver in the light,
Red and green coral tangled in his hair,
The sea the black of the night.

But when the sea is calm,
The bear takes a sleep,
His snores ripple the water,
Which comes and tickles your feet!

All the dangers you could meet
When travelling to me,
Across the wide blue ocean,
Across the wide blue sea,
But stay unharmed, my dear love, please,
My future wife to be.

Jenny Hewlett (11)
Witton Middle School

Life

The grand musical,
the opera, soap, play, show,
the never-ending story.
We all play our assigned roles
and wear smiles as we do it.
Bask in the warm majesty of life,
marvel at the wondrous hues of beauty.
We surround ourselves with nothing that matters.
Be happy,
love one another,
treasure the magic of life,
before it's taken away.

Rosalind Martin (11)
Witton Middle School

The Four Seasons

It was only last spring
When I had my first ring,
It fits like a glove,
It was from my first love!

It was only last summer
When I saw him again,
Heart full of gold,
Though he's gone a bit bold!

It was only last autumn,
We had a big row,
He's gone off me now,
He thinks I'm a sow!

It was only last winter
He phoned me and said,
'You will marry me!'
He's got a big head!

Zoë Cattell (11)
Witton Middle School

Monkeys

Monkeys, monkeys everywhere,
swinging around in the air,
swinging high, swinging low,
swinging as fast as they can go.

Monkeys, monkeys, everywhere,
swinging around like they don't care,
swinging high, swinging low,
swinging as fast as they can go.

Monkeys, monkeys, everywhere,
Would you stop them? Would you dare?
Swinging high, swinging low,
Swinging as fast as they can go.

Amy Grimley (9)
Witton Middle School

School Time Substitute

It's school time again.
Time to settle down to maths.
Here comes Teacher,
Hold on, that's not her!
It's a substitute!
Quick, set the traps!
Pins on the chair!
Tic-tacs instead of tablets!
Fake names in the register,
Rude words on the board!
Give our homework to the fish
And set the hamster free!
Put salt in her tea
And fish food instead of biscuits!
Quick, here she comes,
Sit down and pretend to read!
'Morning, class.'
'Morning, Miss.'
Giggle, giggle.
She reaches for her tea. *Uh!*
She takes a biscuit. *Uhh!*
She looks at the board. *Oh my!*
She asks for homework. *Argh!*
The hamster runs over her shoe. *Eek!*
She sits on her chair. *Oww!*
Ding. School's over.
We enjoyed our day,
But did she?

Andréa Hinton (10)
Witton Middle School

Winter - Haiku

Making a snowman
Lot's of snow for snow fighting
Christmas brings Santa.

Lucy Martin (9)
Witton Middle School

Alien Trouble

Sorry Mum for being bad,
Sorry for zapping Uncle and Dad.
They really deserved it,
For watching that Kermit,
I'm actually so sort of glad.

Sorry Mum for the teleport trick
I know he got really quite sick.
He was being mean
And also so clean,
But then Carl is just plain thick.

Sorry Mum for flying round,
I was only a centimetre off the ground.
I did a loop
And gave a whoop,
I was nowhere near that loud.

Those were only the beginning,
I was only interested in winning.
It was only a dare,
Not a big scare,
I made John go singing.

Frances Baker (10)
Witton Middle School

Great, Great Granny

My great, great gran is 82,
bubblegum she likes to chew.
She goes down town and buys in the shops,
mini skirts and blue crop tops.
She slaps on the make-up, it doesn't take long,
as she hums along to some new pop song.
In her red sports car she races fast,
music on nearly full blast!
She lies in the sun and collects a tan,
she's my great, great, groovy gran!

Katie Harwood (11)
Witton Middle School

The Weird Seasons

It came winter and again,
But it felt more like summer.
The grass grew and the flowers too,
That's why it felt like summer.

When spring came everyone was to blame,
Because the flowers died too early,
People watered them too much,
And that was the end of the story.

Then summer appeared out of the blue,
It was terrible storms and big rains too,
Most people said they were ashamed,
The others said it was a game.

There was an end to all of this,
When autumn came and smelt like bliss,
The leaves were multicoloured and the flowers were dying down,
Finally the villages had enough, so they didn't hear a sound.

Alice Price (10)
Witton Middle School

Christmas

I wish that it was Christmas every day,
Playing with toys and eating lovely Christmas dinners.
The Christmas tree is decorated with pretty lights.
Then when it is Christmas Eve and it is time for bed,
You can't sleep and you're waiting and dreaming about the next day.
You miss the point of Christmas,
It is not all about chocolate and toys,
It is about spending time with your family.
Oh I wish that it was Christmas every day.
Oh I wish it was Christmas every day.
So now I know, I will never forget!

Kara White (10)
Witton Middle School

Spaghetti

Spaghetti, spaghetti, it's so much fun,
It's Italian food
and is nicer than gum.

Spaghetti, spaghetti, all over the floor,
up on the ceiling
and splat on the door.

Spaghetti, spaghetti, it goes everywhere,
all over my face
and sticks in my hair.

Spaghetti, spaghetti, it's my favourite food,
when I eat spaghetti,
I'm never in a mood.

Spaghetti, spaghetti, twisted on my fork,
would you have spaghetti,
or would you have pork?

Spaghetti, spaghetti, I always want more,
when I've had spaghetti,
I shout, 'Encore, encore!'

Spaghetti, spaghetti, with so much stuff,
Bolognese and meatballs,
Not the Billy Goats Gruff.

Spaghetti, spaghetti, it's gone in the end
and when it is finished,
it drives me round the bend.

Isabelle Amos (10)
Witton Middle School

Midsummer Moment - Haiku

Dreamy moment, still
And calm, sweet surrounding, the
Fairy queen lies there.

Sophie Cave (10)
Witton Middle School

The Magic Box

(Based on 'Magic Box' by Kit Wright)

I will put in the box . . .
A roar of a Chinese dragon
The silence of Remembrance Day
The sound of a firework on the 5th of November
The hiss of a snake slithering on the ground.

I will put in the box . . .
A crash of a wave hitting a rock
A moon in the morning and a sun at night.

I will put in the box . . .
A drip of a tap
The opening of a morning glory
The twinkling of the moonlight stars
And the light of a full moon.

I will put in the box . . .
The hair of a unicorn
The scuttle of a spider
A snap of a crocodile
And the giggle of a girl.

I will put in the box . . .
The sound of a bomb
The skeleton of Tutankhamen
And the reload of a gun.

I will put in the box . . .
A bottle of the finest beer
The blink of an eye
The miaow of a kitten
The boots of David Beckham and the colours of a rainbow.

My box is fashioned from
The skin of a snake and the horns of a dragon to open it.
The hinges are made from spider's legs.
I will fly my box in the starry sky, fall through the air
And land on a big bed and sleep through the night.

Bradley Jeans (10)
Witton Middle School

The Flower

It touched me
with its colourful petals
and then it stepped on me.

It kicked me
with its long, curly leaves
and then it stung me.
I looked at my arm,
its sharp thorn sticking out.

I got up
and its head was staring at me.

I watched its stalk shaking,
so when I was running
and running it caught me.

It touched me
with its colourful petals
and then it stepped on me.

It kicked me
with its long, curly leaves
and then it stung me.

Colette Staley (10)
Witton Middle School

All About My Family

My family is nice,
Just like rice.
They are always smiling,
As children are whining.
My grandad is fit,
As my nan sits.
My uncle is always driving,
As my auntie is always rhyming.
My mum is always spending,
As my dad is always mending.

Jessica Keyho (9)
Witton Middle School

Seasons

Oh it is the spring,
How much joy it really brings,
A time of blossom.

Summertime, *hooray,*
Yay, the summer holidays,
Yeah, relaxation.

Autumn, autumn leaves,
Red, yellow, brown and crunchy,
Yes I love autumn.

Now it's the winter,
I like its bitter coldness,
Oh it's winter.

Emma Henley (10)
Witton Middle School

The Train

I am the train
that speeds along the track.
I am the track
that jumps over hills.
I am the hill
that holds the flower.
I am the flower
that relaxes in the light.
I am the light
that twinkles on the station.
I am the station
that holds the track.
I am the track
that carries the train.
I am the train
that speeds along the track.

Sophie Walsh (11)
Witton Middle School

The Television

It looked at me
with its shining screen,
and then it screamed at me.

It screeched at me
with its booming volume,
and then it whispered at me.

I turned it on
with its great big remote hand.

I pulled it over.
It grabbed me!
I hit the button with my hand.

It looked at me
with its shining screen
and then it screamed at me.

It screeched at me
with its booming volume,
and then it whispered at me.

Gemma Oliver (10)
Witton Middle School

The After Eight's Club

What a jolly and fantastic evening!
You can't tell yachts from dolphins leaping
and jumping in the mid horizon.
Having a magnificent time. Seaweed dancing with joy:
the stones and rocks surfing through the waves.
The water crashing to the shore and sucking back to sea,
as the tides dance to the silent tune of the moon.
The bi-valves clap quietly from their roosts
upon the sunken rocks, whilst above their heads,
froth waltzes majestically upon the ridges
of the water.

Emma Houlston (11)
Witton Middle School

I Am The Leaf

I am the leaf
that twirls through the wind.
I am the wind
that strokes the grass.
I am the grass
that guards the flowers.
I am the flower
that spreads the seeds.
I am the seed
that flutters to the ground.
I am the ground
that anchors the tree.
I am the tree
that mothers the leaf.
I am the leaf
that twirls through the wind.

Heather Lamb (11)
Witton Middle School

It's Not Fair!

It's not fair! I never get to play,
even on a sunny day.

It's not fair! I'm always late for places
even though I take big paces.

It's not fair! I have to go to bed at nine,
even when I'm feeling fine.

It's not fair! I have to come back from the park
just because it's getting dark.

It's not fair! I have to set the table for tea,
even though I'd rather watch TV.

Lucy Deakin (10)
Witton Middle School

The Midnight Owl

Owl, owl, with blinking eyes
Swoops making no sounds.
Owl, owl, with feathered wings,
Flies up above the clouds.

Owl, owl, fly far and near,
Fly, fly, low and high.
Owl, owl, gracefully fly
Across the midnight sky.

Owl, owl, fly through the air,
Catch the season's breeze.
Owl, owl, you spot your prey,
Which in your claws you seize.

Owl, owl, fly far and near,
Fly, fly, low and high.
Owl, owl, gracefully fly
Across the midnight sky.

Owl, owl, fly up and far,
Towards the furthest star.
Owl, owl, in the sky you prowl,
My own midnight owl.

Catherine Griffin (10)
Witton Middle School

Haiku

Salmon jump upstream
Joyful children playing ball
Fairies flying by.

Gerallt Wheeler (10)
Witton Middle School

School

School is cool.
For our school
We're on our best,
So we get a test
For no reason.
So we plead them.
We choose a test to do
But that has nothing to do with you.
Teachers are boring,
So we are snoring.
We have to learn
Every term.
That is sad,
So we are bad.
It's come to the end of school.
Half-term!
No more to learn
From the weeks gone by.
So for now, it's goodbye.

Rebekah Watton (10)
Witton Middle School

A Poem For Valentines

Feelings are bright,
Feelings are blue.
Sky is a beauty,
Red is love.
Kindness is white,
Meanings are true to music,
Hearts are for Valentines,
Love is for two
And two is as bright as light.
Yellow is as bright as a daffodil.
Love is for life
And life is for love.

Victoria Ribeiro (10)
Witton Middle School

My New Year's Resolutions

I will always do my homework
Try and get it in on time,
I'll try and be polite to my teacher
And get my poems to rhyme.

I'll tidy my room more often,
And not eat too much food,
I'll stop my cheek to Mum and Dad
And try and stay out of a mood.

I'll try and be a bit more careful
And not be mean to my brother,
I'll learn to change my sister's nappy
And be much nicer to my mother.

I'll try to get to bed earlier
And try not to splash in the puddle,
I'll do the washing up when it's my turn
And try not to get maths in a muddle.

I'll try and paint a picture,
And take my time over it,
I'll try and improve my manners
Just a tiny bit!

Amelia Quiney (9)
Witton Middle School

The Sun

The sun comes out in the morning
And goes back in, in the evening.
It gives us light throughout the day
And when it goes in, it likes to say,
'Goodbye, my friends, I'm going home,
I'll have to leave you all alone.
I'll be back tomorrow in the sky.
Goodbye, goodbye, goodbye.'

Rebecca Gough (10)
Witton Middle School

The Leaf

A leaf falls down off its tree,
It flitters along in wind,
Up and down with other useless things,
No one cares or stares at a poor, helpless leaf.

It trails along the pavement,
Narrowly missing the bags and feet of all the humans around,
Getting swept up the walls and trees,
Trying to cling on.

Banned from the warmth of shops, the leaf was left in the cold,
All crinkled at the sides and rusted looking, it rolled under a foot.
As the feet flattened the leaf its heart skipped a beat . . .
It survived, barely a mark or a scratch.

All of a sudden the leaf was whisked away
And landed in a garden on a compost heap.
It finally got used to the garden,
The leaf was happy in the end and allowed the warmth of the house.

Alex Alderson (10)
Witton Middle School

Best Friend

A real carer
A great sharer
Really kind
A great mind
A CD lender
A text sender
A trendy trainer wearer
A great darer
A secret keeper
A creepy creeper
A boy hater
See you later!

Rachel Claringbull (10)
Witton Middle School

Snowman, Snowman

Snowman, snowman,
Out in the cold
He's got buttons
For eyes and
A mouth
Made of coal.
He hasn't got ears,
He can't see at all,
As cold as an ice cube
Feels like a snowball.
Snowman, snowman,
Where have you gone?
Just about melted away
In the midsummer sun.
Snowman, snowman
Out in the cold,
He's got buttons
For eyes
And a
Mouth made of coal.

Cerise Bartlett (10)
Witton Middle School

The Caterpillar

Little creepy-crawlies, hiding under leaves,
Eating all the flowers,
They're just like little thieves.

Now he's gone away, into his brown home,
It's like he's gone forever
I'm feeling very alone.

Now two weeks have passed, he's shown his head again,
Two wings have sprouted from his back,
He's fit to play again.

Jessica Rollit (9)
Witton Middle School

The Book Of Odd And Strange

Pink cows and blue crocodiles,
Red koalas with polka dot smiles,
Green mice and purple snails,
Yellow kangaroos with striped tails,
Everything's odd and strange,
Why don't we turn the page?

Curtains that are round and walk,
Posters that see and talk,
Mirrors that show different people, not you,
Pencils that sneeze, 'Achoo, achoo.'
Everything's odd and strange,
Why don't we turn the page?

Shoes that jump up and down,
Hats that each wear a crown,
Trousers that run away from you,
Knickers that jump down the loo,
Everything's odd and strange,
Please don't turn the page!

Astra Williams (10)
Witton Middle School

Imagine

Imagine you lay
As long as a sleigh.
Imagine a hen,
Bigger than ten.
Imagine a paw
As big as a door.
Imagine a house
As small as a mouse.
Imagine a cat
That wears a hat.
Imagine this rhyme
As quick as the time.

Matthew Vigurs (9)
Witton Middle School

I'm So Healthy

I'm so healthy
Didn't you know?
I can use my fingers
To touch my toe.

I'm so healthy
Didn't you know?
Fruit is my favourite,
Don't like things made from dough.

I'm so healthy
Didn't you know?
Pizza makes me sick,
What did you say? *So!*

I'm so healthy
Didn't you know?
Here comes healthy head,
Oh no!

Gabrielle Smith (9)
Witton Middle School

Animals That Went Wrong

Over there there's a koala wagging its pink tail,
And over there is a kangaroo wearing a blue veil.
In the corner is a monkey, putting on its dress,
Next to it a gorilla, painting a huge mess.
On my left is a giraffe with a very small neck,
And on my right a hippo, looking a bit of a wreck.
Sitting in the bath, a hamster with a hat,
Up above its head, hanging is a rat.
Swimming in the sea, an elephant with no ears,
Having tea and cake are two purple deer.
Far across the distance a panda is up high,
Wearing matching wings to the colour of the sky.
While my cat in the corner is eating apple pie,
I'm sitting watching the wonders of the world go by.

Daniella Wood (10)
Witton Middle School

The Cider Spider

Jack and Jill went up the hill
To fetch a pail of cider,
When they came down, Jill tripped and frowned
And tipped it over beside her.

Incy wincy spider went up the water spout,
Down came the cider and Incy gave a shout.
He fell down the drain all over again,
What a drunk little lout.

Little Miss Muffet, sat on her tuffet,
Eating a steak gravy pie.
Down came a spider, who started to eye her,
They got married the next July.

The wedding was bliss, there was no crisis,
Jack and Jill were crowned.
Humpty Dumpty got all grumpy
And there was cider all around.

Emily Sparkes (11)
Witton Middle School

Football Mad

Football's fun
Football's great
I play football with my mates

Playing matches every day
Kicking, tackling any way
Watching the ref and making sure
That every match I get to score

I love the kit
I love the game
It keeps me fit
And gives me fame!

Bradley Taylor (10)
Witton Middle School

Friends

Georgina, Alice and Tyler are my friends
We will stay together till the world ends.
We will like each other for ever and ever,
We will never break up with each other.
They're like me and I'm like them,
We are nine, but nearly ten.
We have lots of other friends,
We never drive each other round the bend.
We each have a baby brother,
And a lovely mother.
We like netball,
But not football.
We like clubs,
But not pubs.

Bethany Foden (9)
Witton Middle School

Warning: This Poem Is Extremely Scientific

As I looked around my lab, this is what I found:
A packet of uranium, sold by the pound,
Some citric acid inside a chromatograph,
With complicated readings from a very large seismograph.

And this is what I also found:
A pair of white mice, all safe and sound,
Then there were my papers on exothermic reaction,
Clipped to a report showing molecular interaction.

Ah, there is my Bunsen burner gas,
Now where is my collection of test tubes made of glass?
They're over here by my grubby coffee cup,
My last thought today was that I really need to tidy up!

Russell Black (10)
Witton Middle School